SACRIFICE
THE LEADER

PAUL L. COX

A STRANG COMPANY

Old Testament, R. Laird Harris, ed., Chicago, IL: Moody Press, 1980.

Design Director: Bill Johnson
Cover design by Jerry Pomales

Library of Congress Control Number: 2008929185
International Standard Book Number: 978-1-59979-392-4

08 09 10 11 12—987654321
Printed in the United States of America

This book is dedicated to my parents, Jerome and Phyllis Cox, who trained me up in the Lord, had untiring belief in what I could do, and set me on a platform on which the Lord was able to build.
I thank them for giving me a love for the Word of God and for the church of Jesus Christ. I am the recipient of generational blessings because of their love of Jesus.

CONTENTS

INTRODUCTION

M Y JOURNEY AS a leader began in high school when I was invited to lead a Sunday school class. While I was attending college, I was responsible for the addressograph department of Signal Oil Company. I then served as a counselor at Green Oak Ranch Boys Camp. During the following years I was an eighth grade public school teacher for three years, a full-time youth worker for six years, a pastor for twenty years, and a schoolteacher in a child/adolescent psychiatric ward of a hospital for six months. For the past seven years I have served with my wife as co-director of Aslan's Place.

Over twenty years ago the Lord first planted the seed in my mind for my original manuscript, *Sacrifice the Pastor*. As a Baptist pastor I had experience with individuals who would tell me confidential issues in their lives and then, within a few months, they would either turn against me or leave the church. I realized that in some way I had become the sacrifice for their sins, rather than the Lord Jesus.

Now I understand that this is not just a transaction that takes place with pastors. As compassionate Christian leaders listening to the hurts of others, we can be placed in a position to become a sacrifice. This can happen as businessmen, therapists, schoolteachers, principals, small group leaders, church staff professionals, or simply friends who listen with a kind heart. Therefore, this book is not only relevant for pastors, but also for all those who find themselves in leadership positions—thus the new title, *Sacrifice the Leader*.

I would like to clarify a term we often use in the local church—the word *minister*. We have incorrectly defined a minister as anyone who has met the qualifications of a denomination and is ordained. This is not the biblical definition of a minister. Ephesians 4:11–12 defines a minister as one who has been equipped by apostles, prophets, evangelists, pastors, and teachers to do the work of ministry. Therefore all who are followers of Jesus Christ are ministers. Any leader who is a Christian is a minister. For that reason, whenever I use the term minister in this book, I am referring to all believers, with the focus on those believers who are leaders. Your ministry may be in a church, in a religious organization, in the marketplace, in the education arena, in the government, in the medical community, or at home. It does not matter. Wherever you are, you are a minister. Wherever you minister, you may find yourself counseling. Whenever you counsel, you may find yourself being set up to be a sacrifice.

This book addresses these issues and helps us to keep our focus on Jesus as our only sacrifice. The principles presented in this book will help keep us in unity so that the work of the kingdom of God will progress here on earth.

1
THE LEADER AS SACRIFICE

A SURVEY OF 4,665 Protestant minister leaders showed that 58 percent felt that the work of the church seemed futile or ineffectual. Reverend Roy Oswald, a behavioral scientist and authority on clergy burnout, believes that one of every four clergy is burned out and another 25 percent are under great stress and may be on their way to burnout. Even though no comparable study has been made of the laity, I believe that the feelings of frustration and burnout among the laity parallel those of the clergy.[1]

Pastors who have been in the ministry for any period of time and leaders of all kinds find these concerns familiar. Due to the powerlessness of feeling ineffectual, many grow discontent and reconsider the advisability of a lifelong commitment to a leadership role. After frustrating years of service, many find themselves burned-out and willing to say "goodbye" to their leadership position, which they once considered the one great dream of their lives.

The consequences of this exodus are especially grave—draining the leadership pool of the Christian church. The effect on those who are in leadership positions in organizations and on their families causes deep suffering and results in a silent, private crisis. If any leader is driven to quit, it results in wasted years of preparation and squandering the investment of congregations and educators who helped to support and train them in preparation for leadership. While observers notice this flight from leadership, it also affects young people who are in the process of deciding if they will take the risk of entering any role of leadership in the church or other organizations.

CAUSE FOR CONFLICT

Leaders give up for many reasons. Some struggle with lack of fulfillment. Others feel inadequate and unable to make a difference. Many feel overwhelmed by the unreasonable time commitment required. Each of these elements contributes to discouragement. These conflicts can cause the burden of leadership to feel like an overpowering, crushing weight. Ongoing conflict adds to this heavy burden. When one conflict piles atop another, it can finally compel a leader to call it quits.

Why do conflicts develop between leaders and others? There are probably as many reasons as there are situations. However, a common thread that characterizes many such conflicts may deserve more attention. Can you imagine the conflict when the Christian leader may, as a spiritual leader, bear the weight of sins and become a sacrifice for the unresolved sins of those over whom he has leadership? Once this sin has been deposited onto the leader, that leader is then treated as the sacrifice on the altar. The leader is either consumed as a sacrificial lamb or becomes a scapegoat.

Several years ago a couple called me to intervene in a marital dispute. Fortunately they quickly reconciled, but then lost interest in the ministry. Six months later they turned against me. Their accusations included poor management, poor preaching, and irrelevant worship services. Having been members for decades, their criticisms swayed others. Finally they left the ministry. What happened? I become the sin bearer. They deposited their sin onto me and then chose to separate themselves from their sin.

Prepared for Consequences

Conflicts between leaders and those they lead will continue. When one resolves, another disagreement crops up sooner or later. How will the leader respond? The leader who understands some of the dynamics that take place in this relationship gains strength and steps away from those who crater and dropout. With preparation and increased understanding, the leader prepares for the possible consequences of receiving confidential information.

Since the follower is a companion or co-worker in the struggle, he needs to appreciate the dangers involved in revealing information to a leader. If the follower does not feel forgiven by Jesus Christ, he may desire to place his sin on someone else. The leader could be elected to bear the sin. Awareness of this possibility could prevent disruption in the life of any organization.

Avoid becoming the goat

Understanding and information for protection available in this book:

- To help you gain a biblically based understanding of the human need for a sin bearer in
  the form of a sacrifice or scapegoat

- To help you experience a growing understanding
  of the relevant psychological principles that
  are active when a leader talks with a follower,
  concentrating on those dynamics that would
  increase the possibility of a leader becoming a
  sin bearer

- To offer suggestions on how a leader can help a
  follower not to treat the leader as a sin bearer

Arm yourself

Be armed with knowledge. Inside these pages you will find:

- A study of the biblical understanding of the concept of a sin bearer

- A survey of some of the dynamics that can take place between a leader and a follower

- Practical ways for a leader to avoid becoming a sin bearer

- Steps a leader can exercise when a follower projects his sin

Get answers

In Scripture, the key questions have been answered. These questions and others can be answered.

What is the biblical understanding of a sin bearer?

Why are there two models for a sin bearer in the Old Testament?

Why is Jesus the final sin bearer?

How can a leader help a follower accept the sacrifice of Jesus Christ?

Why does a follower sometimes choose to project his sins onto a leader?

What steps can a leader take to prevent a follower from projecting his sins onto a leader?

How can a leader train a follower to accept forgiveness from the Lord?

How does a follower project his sins onto a leader?

Which interpersonal dynamics set a leader up to become a sin bearer?

How can people be educated to assist others in dealing with sin issues in their lives?

How does prayer help individuals to internalize forgiveness?

Which listening skills should a leader develop in order to avoid becoming a sin bearer?

Understand the language

Be further prepared by understanding the terminology. Here are several terms which will be used repeatedly.

Atonement—the act of satisfaction given for wrongdoing or injury.

Conflict Management—the process of working out a relationship between two or more persons who seek goals that cannot be simultaneously attained under the prevailing conditions.

Forgiveness—to give up resentment or the desire to punish.

Karpman Triangle—a transactional analysis model that sees three roles that are assumed in an interaction or communication that is used to provoke or to invite others to respond in specific ways, thus reinforcing early psychological positions. These three roles are persecutor, victim, and rescuer.

Projection—the process of unwittingly attributing one's own traits, attitudes, or subjective processes onto another.

Defense Mechanism—operates unconsciously, so that which is emotionally unacceptable in one's self is unconsciously rejected and attributed to or projected onto others.

Sacrifice—the act of offering the life of a person or animal, or some object, in propitiation of or homage to God.[2]

Scapegoat—a goat over whose head the high priest of the ancient Jews confessed the sins of the people on the Day of Atonement, after which it was allowed to escape. Within this study, the scapegoat will be seen as a person, group, or thing upon whom the blame for the mistakes or crimes of others is thrust. Following the sin "inoculation," the scapegoat leaves or others try to get away from it.

Script—briefly defined as a life plan, very much like a dramatic stage production that an individual feels compelled to play out. A script is related to the early decisions and the positions taken by a child. It is in the child ego state and is "written" through the transactions between a child and his parents. The games that are played are part of the script. When the positions and games are identified, a person can become more aware of his script.[3]

Sin Bearer—a person, object, or animal on which the sin(s) of someone else is placed. The person or persons on whom the sin or sins is placed is the sacrifice.

Transference—the displacing of feelings from one object or person to another. For example, the client transfers the hatred he feels towards his father onto his analyst.

WHY A SACRIFICE?

The age old question begs an answer: Is there a God-shaped void in all of us? Do all people—regardless of origin—recognize on some level, even a subconscious one, the need for someone to do for us what we cannot do for ourselves? Is sacrifice necessary?

2
IS SACRIFICE NECESSARY?

TWENTIETH CENTURY MAN detests the idea of a sacrifice. The word dredges up images of primitive natives dancing around a fire in some distant jungle. This picture might reveal a man savagely plunging a crude knife into a helpless beast. Red blood splatters over the altar, dripping onto the dark earth. The air fills with pagan cries, chants, and rhythmic drumming.

Some people say the need for a sacrifice is as outdated as primitive man. They would say we have progressed past the need for such an ancient practice. But have we?

During the summer of 1984, a cinematic phenomenon surprised American moviegoers. *E.T.* rocked the box office. The heart-tugging story reveals an "extra terrestrial" who befriends a little boy. Around the office water cooler, people chattered about the movie. Most of them had already seen it two or three times.

E.T.'s journey carries him from beyond the solar system to our planet. His powers marvel ordinary earthlings. He demonstrates love and compassion for man through his relationship with the boy. The film tension builds as the precious boy falls so ill that E.T. realizes he must forfeit his own life to save his friend. E.T. embraces the tough choice, trading his life for the boy's. His death saves the boy.

The film offered more than smashing special effects, a moving story line, and superb acting. Did Americans sense truth in it?

Does someone have to die? Is a sacrifice needed—not only for the boy, but also for every one of us?

There is obviously some connection between E.T.'s sacrifice and Jesus' sacrifice for us. In his book, *The Gospel from Outer Space*, Robert Short draws many parallels between E.T. and Christ:

> Both E.T. and Christ are extra terrestrials coming into the world from the "outside in." Both begin their "adventures on earth" in less than auspicious circumstances—E.T. in a shed behind the home where he takes up residence, Christ in an animal shelter behind the inn. Both are males and nothing to look at. E.T. is positively scary until you get to know him, and Christ in Isaiah's well-known prophesy "had no form of comeliness... there is no beauty that we should desire him" (Isa. 53:2, ASV). Both had miraculous powers of healing and other powers over nature and both are marked by great compassion. Both are hunted down by the reigning ideological authorities and both died at the hands of these authorities and both are resurrected from the dead, appearing first only to their most trusted companions. After E.T. is raised from the dead, there is an "empty tomb" scene. While the authorities believe E.T. to be dead, the children know differently and whisk him away in a van. As they help E.T. down from the back of the van, he is covered in a shroud-like white cloth. When the police finally catch up with the van and the doors were fully open, it was seen to be empty. Before E.T. ascends into the heavens in a spaceship that has returned to rescue him, many of his departing words to his companions, the children, are strikingly similar to the words given by Christ to the disciples. "I'll be right here," E.T. said, fingertip glowing

over Elliott's chest. "I'm with you always," Christ tells his disciples before His ascension (Matt. 28:20)[1]

As with Jesus, the climax of E.T.'s story is his death and resurrection. Christ's sacrifice was essential. In the movie, the sacrifice of E.T. was essential.

SOME LOSE, SOME GAIN

What does "sacrifice" mean? Horace Bushnell emphasizes that to sacrifice is to suffer loss even to dying for someone.[2] Therefore loss is important to sacrifice. However, the loss occurs so that future good may take place. Ancient Romans held to the formula "I gave so that you may give."[3] When someone loses for my sake, then I gain.[4] If someone else does not lose, then I must. I know within my heart this is true.

SOMEONE MUST SUFFER

An argument could be made that people avoid the entire issue of guilt by blaming someone else. John Stott in the *Cross of Christ* thinks through this point by writing:

> Is it fair to blame human beings for their misconduct? Are we really responsible for our actions? Are we not more often victims of other agencies than free agents ourselves and more sinned against than sinning? The whole gambit of scapegoats is ready at hand—our genes, our chemistry (temporary hormonal balance), our inherited temper and temperament, our parents' failures during our early childhood, our upbringing, our educational and social environment. Together these seem to constitute an infallible alibi.[5]

Our attempts to blame others only prove that we know our problems must be dealt with in some way. We realize someone must suffer; someone must be a sacrifice for what we have done.

Paul Tournier, a psychologist and popular writer, believes each of us has this innate understanding of our need for a sacrifice. "The notion that everything has to be paid for is very deeply seated and active within us, as universal as it is unshakable by logical argument."[6] Tournier is not alone in seeing that all pagan and modern men are aware of a need for a sacrifice. Horace Bushnell agrees with Tournier. He writes:

> It will not be denied, or should not be, that pagan nations, all pagan nations, have been ready somehow to erect altars and make suit to their gods by sacrifice. This standing confession of guilt and apostasy from God is about as nearly universal as dress, or food, or society.[7]

In every culture, the need for a sacrifice is evident, as Bushnell suggests. Hindus wash themselves in the Ganges so as to be washed from their guilt. "Think of all the penitents and pilgrims of all religions who impose upon themselves sacrifices, ascetic practices or arduous journeys. They experience the need to pay, to expiate."[8] Don Richardson, a former missionary among the Donies in New Guinea, has also found this need for a sacrifice to be universally held.[9]

The need for a sacrifice not only manifests itself in religious ways, such as a sacrifice on an altar, but also manifests in Greek culture. The significant emphasis on the hero in early Greek culture was more than someone doing a great deed of bravery. Martin Hengel believes the early Greeks were really seeing the death of a hero for the good of the community as a sacrifice for that community.[10] Other peoples, Hengel insists, were not only familiar with this concept of a hero's "self-chosen death" as a vicarious death for them, but also for "voluntary deaths as atoning sacrifices."[11]

If man cannot find someone to be a sacrifice for him, then he will turn on himself and make himself or part of himself a sacrifice. Tournier observes that many physiological and psychological troubles are tied to a semi-conscious sense of guilt that must be redeemed. "Numerous illnesses, either physical or nervous, and even accidents or frustrations in social or professional life are revealed by psychoanalysis to be attempts at the expiation of guilt which is wholly unconscious."[12]

The human need for a sacrifice displays itself in unusual ways. In some countries the bull fight becomes the scene of the sacrifice. The sins of the people are laid on the bull and with the death of the bull the peoples' sins are atoned. So effective are these "services" that Paul Tournier believes there is less neurosis in countries that practice bull fights.[13]

In past times, many countries have held their sacrifices on the dueling field. Two engage in combat. As soon as blood has flowed, honor is satisfied, and the opponents embrace each other (if both have survived).[14] The ceremony has resulted in the discharge of guilt. The services are then concluded.

It seems we all need a sacrifice for our sin and guilt. But, how exactly does the Bible define sin? Which root words uncover its true meaning?

3
WHICH ROOT WORDS DOES THE BIBLE USE TO DESCRIBE SIN?

I F THE DESIRE for a sacrifice reverberates in every culture and in every individual, then what is the great need people feel which requires a sacrifice?

First the Bible defines sin in many ways. Scripture declares: "For all have sinned and fall short of the glory of God" (Rom. 3:23). The Bible uses various terms to refer to sin. Each one reveals a different perspective on the nature of man's rebellion against God. The most common Old Testament term for sin is *chattath* in the Hebrew. *Chattah* is used in Exodus 32:30:

> On the next day that Moses said to the people, "You yourselves have committed a great *sin*, and now I am going up to the Lord, perhaps I can make atonement for your *sin*.
>
> —emphasis added

The cognate term of *chattah* is *chatt* which is used in Psalm 51:9. This term and its cognate occur 700 times in the Old Testament and express the idea of missing the mark or erring.

> Hide your face from my *sins*, and blot out all my iniquities.
>
> —emphasis added

The New Testament equivalent of the word *chattah* is the Greek word *hamartia*. Missing the mark is a voluntary and culpable mistake.[1] We find an example of its use in Matthew 1:21:

> She will bear a Son; and you shall call His name Jesus, for He will save His people from their *sins*.
>
> —emphasis added

Agnoia, another Greek term for sin(s), means "to err or to be ignorant, yet to nevertheless be held accountable." Perhaps this relates to the Jewish practice at Yom Kippur of repenting of known and unknown sins. *Agnoia* is the Greek word translated into "sins."

> But into the second, only the high priest enters once a year, not without taking blood, which he offers for himself and for the *sins* of the people committed in ignorance.
>
> —Hebrews 9:7, emphasis added

In the Old Testament, the Hebrew word *shagag* is translated to English Bible versions as "sin" or "sinned." It means "to err as in the human tendency to go astray or to make a mistake." The word was originally used for sheep that go astray from the flock. It represents error in moral conduct and the person is liable to God for this action as in 1 Samuel 26:21:

> Then Saul said, "I have *sinned*. Return, my son David, for I will not harm you again because my life was precious in your sight this day. Behold, I have played the fool and have committed a serious error.
>
> —emphasis added

Moving over to the New Testament, the word *planomai* is translated as "deceive" in the book of Mark in the King James

Version but "misleads" in the New American Standard Version. It means to be deceived. It is an error or sin which is avoidable.

> And Jesus began to say to them, "See to it that no one *misleads* you. Many will come in My name, saying, 'I am He!' And will mislead many."
> —Mark 13:5-6, emphasis added

The same word is used in this verse.

> Or do you not know that the unrighteous will not inherit the kingdom of God? Do not be *deceived*; neither fornicators, nor idolaters, nor adulterers, nor effeminate, nor homosexuals...
> —1 Corinthians 6:9, emphasis added

A word which appears in the New Testament in Romans 1:18 is the Greek word *asebeia* which means "ungodliness." In the version below, the word *godlessness* is used.

> The wrath of God is being revealed from heaven against all the *godlessness* and wickedness of men who suppress the truth by their wickedness.
> —NIV, emphasis added

The Hebrew word *abar* appears in Numbers 14:41 and means to "cross over" or "pass by." It is translated as "transgression" in the English Bible, but "transgressing" in the New American Standard. The Greek equivalent of the Hebrew word is *parabaino* which appears in Romans 4:15.

> But Moses said, "Why then are you *transgressing* the commandment of the LORD, when it will not succeed?"
> —Numbers 14:41, emphasis added

> For the law brings about wrath, but where there is no
> law, there also is no *violation*.
> —Romans 4:15, emphasis added

William Wilson Old Testament Word Studies defines the
word *awa* as "iniquity, vanity, and trouble." The word seems
to have a special reference to the nature and consequences of
sin, especially idolatry, standing in opposition to the solid good
and happiness which attends true religion. It means to turn the
wrong way, as applied to the distortion of the heart or actions
from that which is right to that which is wrong.

The word *iniquity* applies to the original depravity of man,
by which he is turned aside from the image of God and the love
of holiness. It means "to act in a deceitful, tricking, insidious
manner, bad, dishonest; dealing in secret, or under some cover,
unfair usage, and unrighteousness in judgment."

> You shall do no *injustice in judgment*; you shall not be
> partial to the poor nor defer to the great, but you are to
> judge your neighbor fairly.
> —Leviticus 19:15, emphasis added

In the Old Testament the word *pasha* is translated as "rebel-
ling" or "revolting" in Isaiah 1:2. Revolting against God is sin.

> Listen, O heavens, and hear, O earth, For the LORD
> speaks, "Sons I have reared and brought up, But they
> have *revolted* against Me."
> —Isaiah 1:2, emphasis added

Another word for rebellion in the Old Testament is *marah*
which is translated "to rebel" in Isaiah 1:20:

But if you refuse and *rebel*, You will be devoured by the sword. Truly, the mouth of the LORD has spoken.

—emphasis added

Resha is usually translated "wickedness" in the Scripture. Its root meaning speaks of tossing or restlessness.

But the *wicked* are like the tossing sea, For it cannot be quiet, And its waters toss up refuse and mud. "There is no peace," says my God, "for the wicked."

—Isaiah 57:20–21, emphasis added

In Jeremiah 42:6 the Hebrew word *ra* is translated "evil or unpleasant":

Whether it is pleasant or *unpleasant*, we will listen to the voice of the LORD our God to whom we are sending you, so that it may go well with us when we listen to the voice of the LORD our God.

—emphasis added

In surveying the many words used to describe sin, a common characteristic appears. Erickson, in his *Christian Theology*, notes that "a common element running through all these varied ways of characterizing sin is the idea that the sinner has failed to fulfill God's law."[2]

DEFINING SIN

Having examined the different words describing sin aids us in understanding the definition. Erickson defines sin as "any lack of conformity, active or passive, to the moral law of God. This may be a matter of act, thought or of virtue, disposition or state. Sin is a failure to live up to what God expects of us in act, thought and being."[3]

Bloesch sees *sin* as "positive rebellion, not simply a privation of goodness or being. The essence of sin is unbelief which appears as both idolatry and hardness of heart."[4] Sin entails separation from God as well as a deliberate violation of His will and signifies both a state of alienation or estrangement from God and a transgression of His law. It is a wrong direction as well as wrong acts. It is missing the mark, but even more profoundly it is a fatal sickness."[5]

Sin affects the whole person—the will (John 8:34), the mind and understanding (Gen. 6:5), the affections and the emotions (Rom. 1:24–27), as well as our speech and behavior (Mark 7:21–23).[6] The term most frequently used for this affect of sin on man is total depravity. Total depravity does not mean that man is as base as he could be, but rather that every aspect of his person is affected by sin. Bloesch helps us understand total depravity:

> In the perspective of Biblical faith total depravity can be thought of as having four meanings *all of which are valid. First, it refers to corruption* at the very center of man's being, the heart, for this does not mean that man's humanity has ceased to exist. Second, it signifies the infection in every part of man's being, though this is not to infer that this infection is evenly distributed or that nothing good remains in man. Third, it denotes the total inability of simple man to please God or come to Him unless moved by grace, though this does not imply that man is not free in other areas of his life. Fourth, it includes the idea of universal corruption of the human race, despite the fact that some peoples and cultures manifest this corruption much less than others.[7]

Sin and depravity are defined as being universal. What do we do with this sin?

4

WHAT DO WE DO WITH OUR GUILT?

NOT ONLY IS sin a universal fact, but awareness of our own sin is also a universal experience.

There is no culture or language without some vocabulary to designate man's guilty failing. Everything seems to favor taking the knowledge of sin as the vestibule and point of conduct for the gospel which would then give the answer to this universal problem by speaking of forgiveness and grace.[1]

The effect of sin is also universal in its nature. Because of sin, man recognizes that he is unfit for God's presence, that he is unable to do God's will, that he is unrighteous before God's law, and that he is insensitive to God's word.[2]

One manifestation of sin in a person's life is guilt.[3] The guilt that drives one to desire a sacrifice is the guilt that is "the objective state of having violated God's intention for man and thus being liable for punishment."[4] Violation of God's law has occurred. We, as a people, are not thankful for the kind gifts of a gracious God. We refuse to acknowledge God as God.

We seem to be intuitively aware of our sin and guilt and of our need for a payment to atone for that sin. John Stott clarifies this thought for us:

If human beings have sinned (which they have), and if they are responsible for these sins (and they are), then they are guilty before God. Guilt is the logical deduction from the premise of sin and responsibility. We have done wrong by our own fault, and are therefore liable to bear the just penalty of our wrongdoing.[5]

THE OLD BOOK

So what do we do with our guilt? Who or what can satisfy the need for a sacrifice? In the Old Testament, God provided the instructions for handling the sin of man. God speaking through His prophets of the sins and the need for repentance was not enough. There had to be some way for men and women, boys and girls to visualize atonement—to actually see and understand the cost of atonement. Only then could forgiveness be understood.

For this forgiveness to happen, there had to a "sin bearer." The intention of the sin bearer was:

> …neither to sympathize with sinners, nor to identify with their pain, nor to express penitence, nor to be persecuted on account of human sinfulness, nor even to suffer the consequences of sin in personal or social terms, but specifically to endure its penal consequences, to undergo its penalty.[6]

The Old Testament sacrifice system helps us understand because it illustrates or foreshadows the price of atonement, forgiveness, and reconciliation. These costs are to be accepted by the sinner. If the sinner does not understand and accept the sacrifice, then there is no actual forgiveness of sins. There is no real sense of being forgiven. That person is left to himself to understand and to try to manage his own sin and guilt. In witnessing the sacrifice take place and by accepting it as payment for his sin, he can understand forgiveness of sin, which was paid for by the sacrifice.

There are four great animal sacrifices referred to in the Old Testament which allowed the Israelites to visualize the forgiveness of sins: the burnt offering, the peace offering, the sin offering, and the guilt offering. When any of these sacrifices are offered, it is possible to differentiate its various steps.[7]

- First, there was the "bringing near." This action was so key that the Hebrew word *garab*, meaning "to bring or draw near," became a technical expression with the meaning "to sacrifice." The "coming near" expressed obedience to God.

- Second, there was the "laying on of hands" (Lev. 1:4). Perhaps two different thoughts were intended. The worshiper was identifying himself with the offering and symbolizing the transfer of the sins from himself to the animal (see Lev. 1:14–15, 5:7–8).

- Finally, there was the "manipulation of the blood." The priest would sprinkle the blood of the sacrifice somewhere near or on the altar. The shedding of blood was mandatory. "No forgiveness without blood meant no atonement without substitution. There had to be life for life or blood for blood."[8] Afterwards, the remainder of the sacrifice was discarded.

Now that we generally understand the steps of the sacrificial system used by the ancient Israelites, it is important to examine events of the most holy day in Israel, the Day of Atonement.

Two pictures of the sacrifice on that day are two unique ways of seeing "sin bearing."

If, as we have seen,

- man has an innate desire to find a sacrifice, and

- man is not willing to follow the divine plan for a sacrifice,

- then he is going to try to do it his way—to counterfeit the divine method(s) in order to somehow deal with his sin and guilt.

The two models used on the Day of Atonement then become the two realities that he would duplicate.

On the Day of Atonement the high priest would begin by bathing himself. Following the bath, the high priest would place upon himself plain white clothes that were only worn on that day. Then the high priest would offer a bull for himself and his household. The high priest would proceed by entering the Holy of Holies in the Tabernacle, placing incense on the altar, and sprinkling blood against the face of the mercy seat. Next, the high priest would cast lots over the two goats. One of the goats would be for the Lord and the other would be the scapegoat. (See Leviticus 16:4–8.)

The High Priest took the blood of the "sacrificial goat" into the Holy of Holies to atone for the sins of the people. The high priest then laid his hands on the head of the remaining goat and confessed all the sins of the people of Israel. Literally, all the sins of Israel were placed on the goat's head. The goat was then sent out into the desert. (See Leviticus 16:9–11, 15–17, 20–22.) Do not miss the point here! The two goats are not two different sacrifices. "The two together are described as a 'sin offering' in the singular...perhaps [showing] a different aspect of the same sacrifice, 'the one exhibiting the means, and the other the results of the atonement.'"[9]

Before we can understand the final solution for sin found in Jesus Christ, we should know that the Old Testament sacrificial system was not just a type of the coming reality of Christ's sacrifice on the Cross. This is not to deny that one function of the sacrifice system was to be a type of Christ's death on the cross. Horace Bushnell is correct when he says in his book *The Vicarious Sacrifice*:

> The ancient sacrifices were, no doubt, appointed to be types of the higher sacrifice, or analogies that, when the time is come, will serve as figures, or basis of words, to express and bring into familiar use, the sublime facts and world-renewing mysteries of the incarnate life and suffering death of Jesus. There were no types in nature, out of which, as roots, the words could grow, that would signify a nobler so entirely superstructure as the gracious work and the incarnate mystery of Christ. The only way, therefore, to get a language for him at all was to prepare it artificially; and the ancient method of sacrifice appears to have been appointed, *partly* for this purpose.[10]
>
> —emphasis added

While it is certainly true that the Old Testament sacrificial system can deliver to us many great truths about the meaning of Christ being our sin bearer, it is also true that the sacrificial death of animals in the Old Testament did have a real legal purpose. On this point John Whitcomb is helpful:

> The Scriptures tell us that something really did happen to the Israelite offerer when he came to the right altar with the appropriate sacrifice; and he was expected to know what would happen to him. What happened

was temporal, finite, external, and legal—not eternal, personally and immediately significant, not simply symbolic and/or proper.[11]

THE PERMANENT NEW AND FINAL BLOOD SACRIFICE

Although there was great value to the Old Testament worshiper in the sacrificial system, it was not until the death of Jesus Christ that the world would finally have an irrevocable sacrifice for the sin of man. The pivotal truth is that if Jesus is not recognized as the singular sacrifice for sin, then a substitute will be sought to fulfill the need man has for a sacrifice.

Forgiveness is found at the Cross of Christ. There is no other location. Christ's sacrifice alone solves the problem of sin. God declares there is no other substitute. "He made him who knew no sin to be sin on our behalf, so that we might become the righteousness of God in Him" (2 Cor. 5:21).

JESUS OUR SOLE SACRIFICE

New Testament scripture proclaims Jesus is our sole sacrifice. John the Baptist first introduces Jesus to the crowd as "the lamb of God who takes away the sin of the world!" (John 1:29).

These were not carelessly chosen words. The entire scene appears to be drawing heavily from the "suffering servant" motif of Isaiah 53.

- When Jesus declared He had come "to fulfill all righteousness" (Matt. 3:15), He was declaring Himself to be God's righteous servant who by His sin-bearing death would justify many (Isa. 53:11).

- When the Father's voice from heaven declared Himself well pleased with the Son, there was also identification with the suffering servant of Isaiah 53.[12] Jesus was led like a lamb to the slaughter (Isa. 53:7).

- Jesus testifies that He had "not come to be served, but to serve, and to give His life as a ransom for many" (Matt. 20:28; Mark 10:45). The word *for* in the Greek means "in place of" or "instead of" and clearly teaches the substitutionary concept of Christ's death.[13]

- The Apostle Paul wrote, "Christ redeemed us from the curse of the Law, having become a curse for us" (Gal. 3:13).

- The author of Hebrews identifies Christ as the sacrifice. He tells us that just as man is destined to die once, and after that the judgment, so Christ was sacrificed once to take away the sins of many people; and He will appear a second time, not to bear sin; but to bring salvation to those who are waiting for Him (Heb. 9:27–28).

- Finally, we have the words of the Apostle Peter: "He Himself bore our sins in His body on the cross, so that we might die to sin and live to righteousness" (1 Pet. 2:24).

Bushnell summarizes what the Bible teaches: "The whole Gospel is a texture, thus of vicarious conceptions, in which Christ is represented in one way or another, as coming into our place, substituted for us, and standing in a kind of suffering sponsorship for the race.[14]

On the cross, Jesus bore our sin. We each owe the penalty of our own sin. He loves us and gives Himself for us. "Instead of inflicting upon us the judgment we desire, God in Christ entered into our place."[15] While this is true, man often does not care to acknowledge this fact. Indeed, "man asserts himself against God and puts himself where only God deserves to be."[16] Man tries to handle his own sin and guilt. Man would rather blame others or even suffer rather than agreeing that God through Christ bore our sins on the cross.

Truthfully, we need a sacrifice.

5
SOMEONE NEEDS TO DIE

MAN KNOWS HIS need for a sacrifice, and Jesus is the only qualified sacrifice for man. So, what happens when someone refuses to accept the sacrifice of Jesus Christ?

ABSOLUTE REJECTION

Some people absolutely reject the reality that they need to surrender anything to Christ. They figure there is no God, or, if there is one, He will forgive everyone anyway. They do not bother with an antiquated concept such as Jesus dying on the Cross.

UNACCEPTED FORGIVENESS

Others refuse to completely accept the sacrifice of Christ. These say they believe in the death of Christ for their sin. They may even be regular church attendees. Some of them fill every kind of position in the local congregation. They have a dilemma, however. They do not really feel forgiven by Christ. They have taken their sins to the Cross and then picked them back up and drag them home again. They harbor their sins with great affection. Some are so emotionally crippled that they do not even understand the dynamics taking place in their own lives.

INSINCERE FORGIVENESS

Others have confessed their sin. Perhaps they have even "gone forward" in a church service and prayed with a prayer minister. Maybe they met with a pastor and discussed at length their desire to change. Yet their confession of faith turned out to be disingenuous. Their sin did not receive serious consideration. The confession was therefore shallow and without a real sense of forgiveness. Don Browning expands on this important fact:

> Anything more than just superficial confession will arouse defenses, resistances, and negative feelings. Without a clear understanding of confession as taking place in the context of a battle and victory over man's condition of worth, confession becomes rationalistic, moralistic, and ultimately guilt enhancing.[1]

All of these groups of individuals share a common need to find a sacrifice. The sacrifice may be a person. It may be themselves. Paul Tournier expresses this notion further when he writes:

> Every class in school has its scapegoat, either a pupil, or often, a master; in every workshop and office, in every assembly or family there are scapegoats who give rise to a measure of harmony through the fact that guilt and reconciliation is unloaded upon them.[2]

Leaders meet people from all of these groups. Because of his position and standing, he is in the precarious position of possibly becoming "the alternative sacrifice." Because the leader is in a position of power, the follower may give the leader god-like characteristics. For some, the leader may actually represent God. This is especially true of those who are leaders in a church or religious organization. In some people's minds, who is nearer to God than the Christian leader? Who is purer or holier? Who is better than this leader to become the sacrifice? Martin Adler, speaking of the respect given a Christian leader, reveals in a subtle way how the Christian leader can become the set up for becoming a sacrifice:

> Clergy enable many parishioners to gain relief by venti-lating wrong feelings, by unburdening themselves of guilt-laden thoughts and tension-producing conflicts, and by revealing socially unacceptable actions. The minister's acceptance and support is meaningful, espe-cially since he represents the authority of God and the church.[3]

The Christian leader is often seen as a priest, whether his religious practice refers to him as a minister or a priest. As priest, he is considered to be "without blemish."[4] The allusion to "sacrificial language" is clear. Once a person establishes a Christian leader as one who is worthy to become the sacrifice, then it is a short step to making them the sacrifice, a scapegoat. Writing about a minister, Charles Smith finds no difficulty in identifying a minister as a scapegoat:

> You are in a very real sense, the modern Protestant equivalent of the ancient Jewish scapegoat, upon which the sins of the people heaped expiated. The esteem in which you are held and the more tangible appreciation in the form of salary and emoluments will be directly proportional to your skill in fulfilling this role. A preacher who appears to be getting a lot of fun out of life does not impress the laity as a very good scapegoat.[5]

WHY SACRIFICE THE LEADER?

Why does the leader find himself becoming a sacrifice for someone's sin? Let's look into the field of psychology in order to determine and clearly identify the interpersonal dynamics that occur. The difficult process can begin simply in a leadership relationship with an individual or through therapeutic relationship.

How does this transfer occur? It takes work to discover how a pastor might be raised to hero status. How does this projection occur? How and why does the congregant force his weaknesses onto the pastor? Which counseling theories assist our investigation?

GIVE SIN AWAY

Sigmund Freud first identified transference and recognized its place in therapy. In transference, the patient, at least in this application, shifts repressed childhood feelings and attitudes onto the counselor.[6] He places these feelings on someone in authority. In relation to the pastor, the parishioner may find himself asking, "Does this pastor live up to the expectations I have for an authority figure?—or more precisely a "father figure"? Browning, in *Atonement and Psychotherapy*, elaborates:

> It is becoming increasingly clear that the therapist occupies a representative role. He represents more than just himself…it is obvious, then, that when a therapist successfully implements a relationship of empathetic acceptance, more is implied than simply that this therapist has accepted this client. His acceptance is a representative acceptance.[7]

This process may bring negative or positive feelings. The transference can be complicated. Often it happens subconsciously, so neither the parishioner nor the pastor may be fully aware of the reasons behind the feelings that surface.

The depth of transference is in direct relationship to the strength of a person's ego. Moshe Halevispero believes, "The weaker the ego, the more powerful and terrifying the transfer; the emptier one feels, the more one confers on transference objects omnipotence and magical powers."[8]

A Hawaiian minister told of a lady who accused him of making a pass at her. Many deacons in the church believed the accusation. An in-depth investigation showed that the lady thought that many men were making improper advances—especially when she wore red. When confronted, she revealed these were not actual incidents. They had occurred in her mind. This could be an example of transference between a Christian leader and a follower.

A few years ago a man came to our church for the first time. At the end of the service, he decided to give his life to Jesus Christ. Then he told his full story. He faced a prison sentence for child molestation. His wife bore the guilt and embarrassment of his crime, and she had three small girls to raise. Later, he went to prison. His wife turned to the church for support. She came for counseling regularly and frequently phoned for advice and encouragement. At a woman's retreat, a mutual friend told my wife that the woman was becoming emotionally involved with me through our contact. Although flattering, it revealed transference. She viewed me as a father figure who could make her life work again.

This case of transference is not uncommon. Not only in my ministry, but in ministries everywhere, transference occurs daily. "Pastors [are] a perfect 'set up' for transference, especially as a father figure, both in counseling and in the pulpit."[9]

Richard Hester writes that transference is born in a person's need to find "a hero, a love object."[10] This "set up" can be devastating to both parties. The follower can give god-like traits to the Christian leader who accepts them. Biblically, transference leads to idolatry. "Transference holds out the temptation to heroism, the temptation to be godlike."[11] Paul and Barnabas experienced this in Lystra after they healed a lame man.

> When the crowds saw what Paul had done, they raised their voice, saying in the Lycaonian language, "The gods have become like men and have come down to us." And they began calling Barnabas, Zeus, and Paul, Hermes, because he was the chief speaker. The priest of Zeus, whose temple was just outside the city, brought oxen and garlands to the gates, and wanted to offer sacrifice with the crowds. But when the apostles Barnabas and Paul heard of it, they tore their robes and rushed out into the crowd, crying out and saying, "Men, why are you doing these things? We are also men of the same nature as you, and preach the gospel to you that you should turn from these vain things to a living God, WHO MADE THE HEAVEN AND THE EARTH AND THE SEA AND ALL THAT IS IN THEM."
>
> —Acts 14:11–15

Transference becomes stage one of transforming the leader into the sacrifice. Once a person has consciously or unconsciously made the Christian leader a hero or a god, that leader is in position to become the sin bearer. It is easy for the leader to accept the appearance that he is "the only one" who can deal with the problem. This is hazardous thinking. "When the minister is invited, via transference, to be seen as thoroughly good, right, competent, and Christlike in a pastoral relationship, he is being seduced into the dangerous role of hero."[12]

BLAME ANYONE ELSE EXCEPT ME

Blaming anyone and everyone for our shortcomings is in vogue. "Failure in my life is attributed to others." A television commercial featuring a hospital in Los Angeles endorses this view. The thirty second spot mentions several types of compulsive behavior. They say, "It is not your fault; you are not alone." So, whose fault is it? It is the implied fault of someone else. "Someone else is the cause for everything wrong with me." The process of placing blame and one's personal feelings on others is called *projection*. Muriel James enhances our understanding of projection:

> A projection is a trait, feeling, or bit of behavior which actually belongs to your own personality, but is not experienced as such; instead, it is attributed to objects or persons in the environment and there experienced as directed toward you by others instead of the other way around. The picture of being rejected, first by his parents and now by his friends is one that the neurotic goes to great lengths to establish and maintain.[13]

When we project our weaknesses onto others, we deny our guilt.[14] Someone else must be responsible. Paul Tournier details the lengths we will go to find someone else to blame. "If we do not project our responsibilities upon our wife, our parents, our supporters, we project them upon society, upon the economic system."[15]

Projection onto the Christian leader is the process of *scapegoating*. A person can project his fault onto the leader and then justify leaving the leader or driving him away—banishing him to some wilderness—anywhere but here. This thinking process is flawed, but it does accomplish its twisted intention. Muriel James, who gave us the definition for projection, reveals the goal of projection:

35

The neurotic [now] rejects others for not living up to some fantastic ideal or standard which he imposes on them. Once he has projected his rejection onto the other person, he can, without feeling any responsibility for the situation, regard himself as the passive object of all kinds of unwanted hardship, unkind treatment, or even victimization.[16]

In counseling, the projection begins by the follower identifying with the counselor. This identification grows during the length of counseling.[17] However, transference can begin in a short time. This is due to the nature of transference and the unique relationship of a counselor with his counselee. One can find himself in a counselor's role even in his business office. When the leader assumes the role of a counselor in any situation he is in the position of a set-up for projection.

Identification occurs quickly when a person senses warmth and empathy from a counselor. A Christian leader often communicates warmth and empathy towards those he leads. Early on in their relationship, identification can occur before any counseling begins. As a result, when any counseling begins, identification may have already occurred.[18]

We gain deeper insights into the process of sacrificing the leader by examining two different personality models: the Transactional Analysis Model and the Systems Theory Model.

6

WHY DO PEOPLE ACT THAT WAY?

TRANSACTIONAL ANALYSIS MODEL

THE TRANSACTIONAL MODEL of personality believes a person is composed of three ego states: Parent, Adult, and Child. The Parent part of the personality contains beliefs and attitudes formed as a result of outside influences, mainly parents. The Adult is a part of the personality that relates to the current reality. "It is organized, adaptable, intelligent, and functions by testing reality, estimating probabilities, and competing dispassionately."[1] The Child is in a state people revert to when they feel, think, and act as a child. An example would be when one looks down and pouts while being chided by a boss. The parent, adult, child role model can be compared with the psychoanalytic counseling theory.

In Freud's concept of the personality, the id could be compared with the Child:

> The id exists to stimulate the organism's basic need and drives (instinct) and to provide for the discharge of energy produced by contact between the organism and the external or internal environment (pleasure principle). Through this mechanism, tension can be released by impulsive motor activity and image formation (wish fulfillment).[2]

The ego could be the Parent. The ego strives to strike a balance between the needs of the id and the super ego. In conjunction with the real world around us, the ego brings the mental images formed by the id into reality.

> The super ego could be compared with the Adult function in transactional analysis. [The super ego is] composed of two parts—the ego ideal (the ideal rather than the real) and the conscience (developed from child's concepts of parents and/or other influential individuals moral inclination)—Super ego is, in essence, a person's moral standard, often thought of as the judicial branch of the personality. The super ego can act to restrict, prohibit, and judge conscious actions. Unconsciously, the super ego can also act, and the unconscious process of the super ego will often lead to detrimental forms of human behavior.[3]

The Child consists of early feelings, responses, and experiences of infancy and childhood. It is expressed as childlike behavior.

When two people relate to each other, there is a transaction. The goal of relationship should be Complementary Transaction.

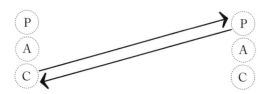

During this transaction, a person receives the expected response to his comments.[4] There are two additional possible transactions, both of which lead to difficulties in the relationship. First, Crossed Transaction occurs when an unexpected response is made.

An inappropriate ego state arises and the lines of transaction between people are crossed.[5] These Crossed Transactions often lead to misunderstanding, hurt, and angry feelings.[6] Second, Ulterior Transactions are transactions that function on more than two levels at a time. In other words, the transaction gives a double message.[7] On the Adult level, I may ask, "Would you like to go to the movies?" However, in the Child state I may really be saying, "You better go with me to the movie!" The second message is usually more accurate although the message sender may deny the intent.

According to transactional analysis, people play nonverbal games with each other. These "games prevent honest, intimate, and open relationship between the players. Yet people play them because they fill up time, provoke attention, reinforce early opinion about self, and fulfill a sense of destiny."[8] The games are played according to scripts which are the discussions and positions taken by the Child. In the game, three distinct roles can be assumed: victim, persecutor, rescuer.[9]

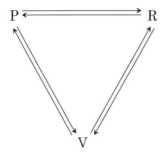

A person can take on one or more of these roles during a transaction, often shifting back and forth between one and the other. Since we understand the basics of transactional analysis, we can look at how this model can help us understand how a pastor becomes a scapegoat.

Why should it surprise anyone when a pastor, like anyone else, gets caught up in the "games" people play? A parishioner may enter into the counseling office where the pastor is seated, fully expecting an innocent conversation will transpire. However, this time it is not so. The follower has already assumed a role and will transfer one or more roles upon the leader. Let the games begin! We cannot exhaust all the possibilities of this encounter between a leader and the follower. But here are a couple of examples.

The follower often enters into a counseling arena seeing himself as a victim. He looks for someone to rescue or to persecute him. The leader may identify the follower's wrong way of thinking and offer a way out. When this happens, the leader moves from persecutor to rescuer. The follower, if not interested in the leader's solution, may feel dissatisfied and rejected. Then the follower turns on the leader, convincing himself he has become the leader's victim. This example is taken from life in a church.

As a victim, the parishioner has entered into a power-less or helpless role. The victim's powerlessness is overt. The powerlessness of the Rescuer and Persecutor are not obvious. They appear to be strong because they have the ability to hurt another person; yet, they too are like the victim in the sense that they are bound together in a pathological triangle. They are helpless to behave in more constructive ways. They are unable to fulfill their needs for growth and change. By considering the different levels of their behavior it is possible to understand how such a complex system operates paradoxically.[10]

The complex process continues. The follower, who sees himself as a victim, turns and becomes the persecutor—making the leader the victim. This is called scapegoating. If the leader is insecure, lacks self-confidence or has a poor self image, he is sucked into the triangle and becomes a more active participant in the game. In the original "set-up," the triangle dealt with the family members, but now the leader has become part of the interlocked process. Originally, scapegoating may have taken place within the family structure. For example, the children could have been scapegoats. Gerald Weeks in Paradoxical Psychotherapy helps us understand this process:

> First, scapegoating may mask marital discord. The tension between the parents may be directed toward or discharged to a child without the parents realizing that the problem is theirs. Secondly, the scapegoat may be used by the parents for their acting-out of stored hostility and covert dependence. On a deeper level, scapegoating may interlock with the unresolved conflicts of separation and maturation the parents experienced with their families of origin. Finally, the cooperative scapegoat may have the covert approval

of the family as a good and loyal family member. In any event, scapegoating is an attempt to balance the system.[11]

The leader has been entangled in the triangular web. Once inside the web, he may become the scapegoat in order to help solve the conflicts in the family structure. The leader then becomes the sacrifice.

A leader can be entangled in the game called "stamp collecting." A person comes into a formal or informal counseling situation with a bag full of stamps or hurts. These hurts, real or imagined, have been collected over a period of time. Each can be redeemed in an instant—especially when his resentment has peaked. "The person redeems his trading stamps by hurting himself, flunking a test, striking out at someone, sitting and brooding,"[12] and by giving himself "a free blowup, drunken binge, suicide attempt, or some other script milestone."[13] Counseling is the perfect location for stamps to be redeemed. If the person does not get the desired response in the counseling setting, the stamps will be redeemed at the leader's expense. The leader becomes the sacrifice—the scapegoat.

One example comes when a person's thinking is distorted by the contamination of the Adult ego by the Parent and/or Child. "Contamination can be thought of as an intrusion between the Parent ego state and/or the Child ego state into the boundary of the Adult ego state."[14] When this occurs in a counseling situation, the leader can once more be set up to become a sacrifice.

> [The person may] exhibit uncontrollable behavior when his sore points are touched....When something rubs the sore spot, the injury may break with an outpouring of strong irrational emotion. A lesion is manifested by a gross overreaction to the reality of the stimulus.[15]

The outpouring of anger is another attempt to make the leader a scapegoat. The person reaches an impasse because the outburst of anger does not work. This inadequate solution only causes other complications. William Hulme notes:

> Scapegoating as an outlet for anger only increases anger. The brutality in scapegoating indicates that this need to afflict pain on another, once it is met, only wets the appetite for more cruelty. This pattern holds true whether our scapegoat is the clergy, (for our anger towards God), or a member of the family, (for our job frustrations), or ourselves, (for our anger towards others). Once the process of scapegoating begins, the dynamics are set in motion for accelerating this destructive bent.[16]

This flailing of emotion at the leader functions differently than the same behavior towards a professional counselor. A professional counselor may witness a response to anger and then not see a counselee for a week. A leader may remain in community with those who have become enraged. For example, the person might see the leader in a social setting following the display of fury. How will that person respond to this leader who knows more about him than others? Now the leader is "set up" to be a sacrifice.

SYSTEMS THEORY MODEL

Systems Theory is defined as follows:

> A system is a set of interacting units with relationships among them. Such relationships include both struc-ture and function. Structure refers to the organization of the unity that consists of subsystems as well as sub

subsystems. Process refers to change in the structure over time.[17]

This theory founded by L. V. Bertalanffy looks interesting. It is practical when working with children and adults who have ongoing conflicts with parents. The total system of a person's life must be understood before help can be given.

The Systems Theory model sees the family as a unit. Where other systems of counseling use individual components as parts that need to be analyzed, Systems Theory says what must be dealt with is the interaction of the components.

In *Peoplemaking*, Virginia Satir says you can take yeast, flour, sugar, and water and make bread. The bread isn't really like any of its ingredients, but consists of them.[18] Self-esteem plays an important part in Satir's system. She sees self-esteem as the basic human drive. In Systems Theory the husband and wife are key to success or failure in the system.

The system is dysfunctional if the husband and wife are not functioning well and they turn to the child to meet their needs. Low self-esteem will result in an unhealthy communication pattern. Virginia Satir identifies those people who do not communicate clearly as the placater, the blamer, the computer, the distractor, and the leveler.[19]

Here is her breakdown:

- *The placater* is one who will do whatever it takes to keep the other person from getting mad.

- *The blamer* is the one who is the faultfinder, the director, and boss. These persons do not feel very good about themselves. They may feel lonely and unsuccessful and attempt to compensate for these feelings by trying to coerce others into obeying them so they can feel that they are someone.[20] This is the kind of person who would say, "After all I have done for you, how could you do this to me?"

- *The computer* is one who is very calm, correct, and shows no feelings. He pretends there is no conflict. These are very reasonable people, and their body language would reflect rigid personalities. He would say nonverbally to the other person, "I am cool, calm, and collected."[21]

- *The distractor* is a person who will make statements that are completely irrelevant to what is going on. He changes the subject and never makes a response to the point. This person is one who evades the issue. What they are really saying is, "Maybe if I do this long enough, it will really go away."

- *The leveler* is one who tries to communicate his honest thoughts and feelings in a straightforward manner. The body language, the voice, and the content of the message all reflect an honest communication of what is being felt. The leveler establishes a relationship that is easy, free, and honest, and this person's self-esteem is not easily threatened. When the leveler responds, there is no blaming retreat into a less desirable form of communication. When apologies take place, one is apologizing for an act, but not for his existence. The leveler understands there are times that he needs to be criticized and evaluated, and times he needs to criticize and evaluate others. "The leveling response is real for whatever it is…it represents a truth of a person at a moment in time. It is whole, not partial. The body sense, thoughts, feelings are all shown and there is integration, a pulling and an openness."[22]

Using the basics of Systems Theory, how can this teach us how a leader might be set up to become a sacrifice? If there is a great deal of low self-esteem in the husband and wife, and if the leader also belongs to a family where there is low self-esteem, then there is a great potential for a "set up." The leader is likely to become part of the person's family system. Because of close emotional ties between a leader and a person or a family, he might entangle himself in the person's dysfunctional family system.

Satir identifies the person communicating in this distorted way as a blamer. The blamer would certainly function in a set up with a leader. The leader could be blamed for the faults of that person or others in the family system. In the process, the leader becomes responsible for the family defects.

This often occurs when a leader works with youth. If a teenager goes astray, it is because the youth leader has not done a good job. If the religious organization had a better worker or a better program, the child would not become rebellious. Once this occurs, the leader is set up to be the sacrifice. Whatever is blamed on the leader is probably not the real problem. The real problem still exists in the family system.

7

THE SET UP: A READY SACRIFICE

W E'VE EXAMINED HOW some persons deal with their guilt by sacrificing the leader. But the leader also plays a part in this conflict as he faces struggles which permit him to be set up as the ready sacrifice.

EXPECTATIONS AND SELF-ESTEEM

After completing several studies of leaders who are pastors, Ed Bratcher, a pastor in Manassas, Virginia, concluded that low self-esteem is the number one problem that adversely affects ministers.[1] A *Leadership* magazine survey disclosed low self-esteem to be a serious problem with the clergy. Of 119 listed difficulties, the responders said stress, frustration, and feelings of inadequacy were of major concern.[2] In yet another survey of 300 Minnesota clergy, the most significant stresses mentioned were time management, feelings of self-doubt, and struggles with one's worthiness for ministry. Even those who were satisfied with their work and enjoyed the support of their congregation wrestled with low self-esteem.[3] This low self-esteem is not just confined to those in the clergy. Pastors are not the only leaders who wrestle with poor self-esteem. Leaders in all types of organization also fight the battle on inadequacy.

So what causes low self-esteem? First a leader is merely a fellow human being. He can experience feelings of inadequacy. Negative thinking can result in depression.[4] A leader can become overwhelmed with the responsibilities of his or her position. In an age of specialization, the leader can become overwhelmed with all that he needs to know. A pastor can especially feel this way because as he relates to those who are specialists, he realizes how little he knows. "He feels like an amateur in a world of professionals, especially if he has been reared in a rural situation or has been trained in a seminary where the rural model is the base model."[5] His self-esteem suffers.

George Anderson, reporting on a poll of Episcopal clergy members, summarizes the frustration the Christian leader feels. "The clergyman is faced with a role in which he finds himself faced more and more often with the question: not how he is able to perform well or adequately, but how is he able to perform at all."[6]

At times the leader may feel overwhelmed with his or her work. "People will come to him and expect knowledge and competence which he does not possess. Consequently, he may receive an almost daily reminder of his inadequacy."[7] Often the expectations of others can be overwhelming.

Who could possibly, for example, fulfill the following job description of a pastor found in Edward Bratcher's book *The Walk on Water Syndrome?* Again, many Christian leaders who are not pastors find themselves in the same position listed below:

He must be a perfect moral example.

He must provide moral and emotional support at all times regardless of his own condition.

He must be an able administrator both in the church and in the community.

He must be an able public speaker on any and every topic.

He must perform as an actor to keep people on the edge of their seats. (i.e. funerals, weddings, picnics, baptisms, etc.)

He must serve as a philosopher, a teacher of values.[8]

Is it not surprising that ministers and other leaders may feel uneasy about these expectations. However, the expectations list goes on. Even the titles assigned to Christian ministers scream of high expectations.

Once [ministers] are ordained, they become not persons but "pastors" or "fathers" or "rabbis" or "sisters" that is, figures in some way standing over others in judgment or authority or sanctity. They are anything but friends, men, women, peers.[9]

If that doesn't cause him caution, perhaps his attitude should. At times, the expectations lie within his thinking process. "The [Christian leaders] suffer terribly from this need to be what they feel they should be, that they know [persons] expect them to be, that they know or feel themselves to be. They know their people expect them to be devout."[10] Even though a person may not expect these qualifications of their leaders, he may feel the leader does and these feelings can lead to loss of self-worth.

Another stress point is the loss of community prestige. Not long ago leaders in the Christian church were held in high esteem. Their presence was welcomed and their advice sought out. But this is not generally true today. "Ministers just are not respected as they once were."[11]

A pastor as a Christian leader is often confused by his perceived position among church members. This can affect his self-esteem. The problem stems from a fuzzy conception of who employs him or her.

A minister's client is both an individual and a congregation—a congregation which changes from month to month, whose members come and go, in response, partly to the satisfaction they derive from his work. The minister has no clear contract with his clients as do other professionals. He is not hired for a definite period but for an uncertain array of services....Unlike a doctor or lawyer, whose clients contract to follow his prescriptions or counsel, the minister's clients can take it or leave it. Moreover, they sit in judgment on him.[12]

Feelings of ineptitude allow the leader to be set for sacrifice.

WHATEVER IT TAKES

The leader who feels poorly about himself may do whatever it takes to prove his worth. In order to show he is capable, he may readily accept the position of the sacrifice, not recognizing the process or where it will take him. He may start down this unsafe path out of a desire to please others and to find worth in himself.

THE INNOCENT FEELING GUILTY

Next, the false guilt the pastor feels can create flaws in his thinking processes.

Once he begins to feel guilty, he may become trapped in an illusion that makes the guilt appear valid. Such illusion can be powerful. He reasons:

1. I feel guilty and worthy of condemnation. This means I've been bad.

2. Since I am bad, I deserve to suffer.[13]

Burns calls this flawed thinking cognitive distortions. In his book *Feeling Good,* he gives several examples of flawed thinking.

All or nothing thinking. Here the person sees himself as either a winner or a loser. There is no in-between.

Over generalization. If one bad thing happens, then other bad things will happen.

Mental filler. The person picks up one negative situation in any event and dwells on it explicitly.

Disqualifying the positive. Here the person turns any positive into a negative. For example, if a compliment is given, one might respond "They're just trying to be nice."

Something bad is going to happen.

Emotional reasoning. Since I feel bad, I am bad.

Magnification or minimization. Here a person either minimizes or magnifies in an effort to make one continue to feel bad.

Should statements. Here the person generally says I should or I must, therefore putting pressure for resentment.

Labeling and mislabeling. The person creates a completely negative self image based on one's error. Extreme over generalization is important at this point.

Personalization. He may assume responsibility for a negative when there is no basis for doing so. He arbitrarily concludes that what happens was his fault or reflects his inadequacies.[14]

What better way to suffer than to become the sacrifice?

THE CONFLICT

Third, when the leader feels confused about his role, he is an easy set-up for conflicts with others. Donald Smith clarifies for us how confusion over role identity increases the likelihood of conflict.

> Role conflicts are likely to be most harmful when role senders are very close to the focal person, are depending upon him, have power over him, and exert pressure on him. Most, if not all, of these conditions prevail in the relationship of many pastors to their church officers. Kahn found that when conflict occurs under these conditions, the typical response of most people is to withdraw either behaviorally or psychologically. This may relieve the stress temporarily, but in the long run, withdrawal is likely to prove self-defeating since it leaves the conflict unresolved and, as we shall see, often causes a series of other related conflicts.[15]

POWER STRUGGLE

Power struggles can develop in any organization. The following survey of twenty congregations showed the most significant problems that people in a congregation had with their leadership. This list can apply to any organization!

- spoke down to us

- did not have head and heart together

- was pious

- was hypocritical

- was lost on a mountaintop

- did not live the gospel in his own life

- treated congregation like children[16]

These responses show a real problem with leadership in ministry. There seems to be a real problem with leaders exhibiting pride and the abusive exercise of authority or power. What led to the overuse or abuse of power by the leaders?

Oddly enough, expectation may be the main reason leaders assume too much power. While all humans desire power, there is good reason for this expectation of many leaders. The biblical qualification for leadership shows us how much we expect of our leaders. The Levitical law requires that no blind, lame, broken-footed, scabbed, or man with any other such blemish should come to the holy place of the Tabernacle. (See Leviticus 21:20.) Only the best could become a priest. The New Testament also holds high ideals for those who would be in leadership.

> [They] must be above reproach, the husband of one wife, temperate, prudent, respectable, hospitable, able to teach, not addicted to wine or pugnacious, but gentle, peaceable, and free from the love of money. He must be one who manages his own household well, keeping his children under control with all dignity...and he must have a good reputation with those outside the church,

so that he may not fall into reproach and the snare of the devil.

—1 Timothy 3:2–4, 7

These high standards are necessary to protect the quality of the leadership in the Old Testament tabernacle system and later in the church. We cannot argue with the sincerity of such regulations. The work of the Lord in any area requires the best. However, such high standards tend to separate the leader from the follower. It becomes natural for a leader to sense any high calling and act with the perceived authority of whatever office he holds.

In *Conflicts of the Clergy*, Margaretta Bowers quotes Catherine de Hueck's views of a priest. The New Testament is clear that we are now all priests! Therefore any Christian leader may sense the expectations of the following words:

> For a priest is a miracle of God's love to us; a man who, through the Sacrament of Ordination, became another Christ with powers that are beyond human imagination…nothing can be greater in this world of ours than a priest. Nothing but God Himself. A priest is a holy man because he walks before the face of the All Holy.[17]

Since the Reformation did away with these sentiments, Protestant leaders are no longer viewed with such admiration. Even though a Protestant minister is not considered to dispense the grace of God, there is still a sense that a minister is "more holy" than others. The same expectation is often applied to any leader.

I visited a family in a small town in Idaho. A young boy played near the family car. He saw the pastor come to visit. "Hi,

God," he said. The boy's words embarrassed and even terrified me. I quickly corrected that misunderstanding.

The lesson sank in. People perceive leaders as different. Several years ago a church leader reinforced the lesson. I went to the church on my day off dressed casually. In the office, a deacon said, "Hello," and scanned my clothing. "Wow! I can't believe you're wearing jeans." The implication sounded clear. Leaders are different. They should not wear jeans.

The pastor as a leader seems to suffer from especially high expectations. Bratcher helps us to understand the tension a church member faces when he thinks about his pastor.

> It is hard for the layman to accept the sinfulness of his pastor. The saints seem superhuman. Intellectually, he can accept the fact that his pastor is a sinner. He's a human being just like us, he says. But to accept that emotionally is another matter. Most of us would like to think that there is someone around better than we are. The likely candidate for this position is the minister. As one church councilman put it, "I know my pastor takes a drink; in fact, I like him to have a drink with me. I know he is married and therefore that he does—well, certain things. This is all fine and dandy. But, doggone it! I still want him to be up there." As he said this he gestured with his hand slightly above his own head. "I want my minister to be a cut above me."[18]

A religious person needs someone who truly represents Christ. Louis McBurney explains this need:

> [They have] the need for an omnipotent, benevolent father; an expression of the all American trait of hero worship; the desire for a personal high priest; . . . [he wants] commitment to Christ by proxy.[19]

How easy it is for the leader to fall prey to such expectations and to readily accept this position?

The minister has to face these expectations. Meanwhile, many in leadership desire to be all others want them to be. For some this means they must be more perfect than even God expects them to be.[20] The counseling role of the Christian leader is an example of how this happens.

> Counselees may demand miracles that the clergy cannot perform. The counselees may set it up this way. You are the representative of God. God is all-powerful and if you really represent Him, you'll solve the problem. And the clergyman feels that he should be able to solve it.[21]

The leader's imperfections position him to accept the power conferred on him. Bossett in *Creative Conflict Administration* reports a study by Harold Lasswell that indicates that people who have unusually high power drives are insecure of their own self worth. "They compensate for this inadequacy by attempting to dominate others. They need to control in order to satisfy a basic need of self worth and power."[22] The study concludes that such insecure persons cannot be good leaders for their need to dominate makes them ineffective.

This kind of person is pleased to be on the pedestal. "Sometimes pastors seek and cherish the pedestal as a defense mechanism against unresolved developmental needs, i.e. independence, authority, and control...[or there may be] latent childhood development problems."[23] At other times it is simply the arena in which the pastor works that leads him to possess this power. "Time pressures, role conflicts, frequent moves all contribute to the assumption of power."[24] A busy schedule can be seductive. One who is a capable leader can always find more to do! The more there is to do, the more likely the leader will deny his limitations. Commenting on this point, Leroy Aden does not appear to deal kindly with Christian leaders. But, the truth hurts.

> We act as though we are or should be beyond the frailties of human existence. It seems to come to us as a surprise that we should become ill, that we should doubt, that we should have discouragements, or that we should have personal or family problems…We find it hard and very uncomfortable to accept our own clay-like existence.[25]

The leader's station as an authority figure can entice him to assume too much power. As a speaker, especially, he pronounces the "word of the Lord," and who will interrupt? As a righteous person, he condemns sin. Is not that his duty? As an administrator, he makes countless decisions that affect the daily course of events in the office. Who better to manage the business of the office than the leader? Bratcher clearly understands the tendency of the Christian leader to go for the power!

> Because a minister is an authority figure, he may become autocratic in his relationships. He may fall into the trap of assuming that his every wish should be viewed as a pronouncement from Mt. Sinai. Moreover, the minister is often encouraged to be autocratic.[26]

Jay Kesler, past president of Youth for Christ, is blunt in assessing what happens in the mind of the minister when power is within reach.

> At times, we are tempted to be Christ, and we feel a compulsion to live as perfectly as He lived. When we see sin in others, we condemn it or forgive it rather

than let Christ do it. We dispense grace rather than participate in it.[27]

Often the leader, in assuming a stance of power, will not admit to having any needs. He must be strong for others and they cannot see him the least bit weak. Louis McBurney, while counseling in the Mayo Clinic, noted that the ministers he worked with expressed this fear of revealing their humanness.[28] It would appear that those attitudes only set up the pastor for a fall, often with serious consequences.

Some leaders, frankly, have a controlling personality. They must be in charge. To be controlled would make the leader vulnerable and for many leaders this is unthinkable. The words of Richard Foster in his book *Money, Sex, and Power* reveal the nature of power in general, but unfortunately speak particularly of a Christian leader.

> For us, it is never enough to enjoy good work. No, we must obtain supremacy, we must possess, we must conquer. The sin of power is the yearning to be more than we are created to be. We want to be gods.[29]

Foster points to the root of the issue of power. We want to control, to be in charge, to determine the course of our destiny and that of others around us. When placed in a position that allows us to do that, we go for it; we go for the power.

Once at this very brink of power we need to evaluate what is taking place in our lives. Richard Foster continues by warning us as we face the demons of power.

> In the desert, we are stripped of all of our support systems and distractions so that, naked and vulnerable, we face the demons without and within. There in the desert, alone we look squarely into the face of the seductive powers of greed and prestige. Satan tempts

us with fantasies of greed and prestige. Satan tempts us with fantasies of stature and influence. We feel the inner pull of these fantasies because deep down we really do want to be the most important, the most respectable, the most honored. But in time we see through the deception. With a power given from above we shout "No" to him who promises the whole world if we will only worship him. We crucify the old mechanisms of power—push, drive, climb, grasp, and trample. We turn instead to the new life of power—love, joy, peace, patience, and all the fruits of the spirit.[30]

This struggle with power is the perfect set-up for the leader to become the sacrifice. When others see the leader as "god-like" and the leader himself enjoys the power that comes with the position, the dynamics are in place. When a person, unwilling to deal with sin in his life, has a conversation with the leader, he may feel that here is one who can take the blame. Whether this person understands the process of transferring his failure or not, the leader becomes the hero that he needs. That person now projects his sin and transfers all blame from himself to his pastor. The leader, already willing to be all that the person wants him to be, eagerly assumes as much power as he can. The leader then effortlessly accepts the role thrust upon him. The leader becomes the sacrifice. It appears that all the participants are content with the transaction.

It is possible for a leader to remain strong despite a person's desire to make him a sacrifice. While there is no guarantee that such strength will prevent the transfer of sin from the person, the leader can assume there is hope. If the leader is strong, not in power but strong in love, healing can take place.

Browning in *Atonement and Psychotherapy* describes the feelings of a client towards his counselor. Note how there is strength without controlling power. "But you were always there like a firm rock which I beat upon to no avail and which merely said your love did not control me and I could not control it."[31] It was this firmness and the therapists' behavior, a firmness to remain constant like a rock, which helped the client eventually find healing.

STRUGGLING WITH STRESS

Stress is another factor that sets the leader up for sacrifice. Samuel Bradshaw observes that stress is a common feature of a leader's life. His findings resulted from a survey of 140 ministers.[32]

In another survey of 4,908 ministers in twenty-one denominations, seventy-five percent reported one or more periods of "major stress" in their careers. Two-thirds of them revealed that the stress was severe. Two out of three times the source of the stress was identified with a ministers' effort in the local church.[33] The causes of the stress were role demands, pressures for perfection, pressure for community leadership, the tendency towards a masochistic martyrdom, and the loneliness a pastor feels as he carries out his duties.

This is not to say that pastors are wholly unsatisfied with ministry. Susan Harrington Devogel in her article "Clergy Morale" also reported that of 300 pastors who responded to a survey, ninety percent felt positive about the ministry and ninety-six percent felt their congregations were supportive.[34]

The pressures that lead to stress, as Bradshaw has noted, can come from many sources. Often, the stress comes from expectations of others or from personal expectations. The leader can always find more to do. Without careful self-monitoring, any leader can turn into a workaholic.

Leaders are taught to be goal oriented. Many set unrealistic goals. When these goals are not achieved, they may experience frustration[35] and subsequently drive themselves harder, often adding more goals to the list of already unaccomplished goals. More hours are needed to accomplish these goals and the stress increases. The nature of ministry complicates this. Goals are to be reviewed to see if they have been reached. But, how do you evaluate ministry goals? How can you chart the change in someone's life? The indistinct nature of these accomplishments only fuels the fire of additional stress. The minister longs to put a handle on his achievements. Perhaps this is why so many pastors talk of the number who attended church last Sunday, the size of the youth group, the number of home Bible studies they have throughout the city, the amount of the church budget, with particular emphasis placed on the dollar value of the mission program, and the size of the past, present, or future building program. Here, at least, there is some measurable way of evaluating if those self-imposed goals are being reached. However, success is never in reach. There is always someone else who has more attending his church, some other church that has a bigger budget, a friend who has a larger staff, and a neighbor who has a media ministry while you do not. The pastor may therefore be frustrated and experience stress.

Leaders who are in ministry are often more susceptible to stress because many tend to be people who operate more on the feeling level than on the thinking level. In a survey of data from the Myers Briggs Type Indicator, it was found that clergy were more likely to choose at the feeling level rather than the thinking level by seventy-nine percent to twenty-one percent. In the general populate fifty percent for each level exists. William Hulme, a professor of pastoral counseling, comments on these findings:

> Clergy as "feeling people" are considerate of other's feelings, understanding of their needs, and predisposed toward conciliation. Yet these qualities can also be problems when one needs to be more objective,

reasonable, and critical—qualities associated with the thinking person….Because clergy tend to make their choices on the basis of feeling, they may too easily give in to conciliation when firmness is needed. The need to please overrules the need to exercise what is currently called "tough love."[36]

This tension of being what a leader should be, versus what he wants to be, clearly adds to his stress level. Stress sets us up to become vulnerable. When a person is under stress, thinking is not as clear and decision-making is hampered. A person under stress is tired, perhaps run down. Often emotions are not as fully under control as when one is rested and not under constant pressure. If a pastor becomes stressed out, he is in the perfect place to be set up as a sacrifice.

An analogy can be taken from the sport of tennis. After several sets of tennis are played, the one who is able to remain calm and collected and yet still continue the drive, despite fatigue, will be the one who will win. The one who falls to the pressure and deteriorates under the fatigue will find it difficult to succeed. Likewise, a pastor who is under constant strain will find it difficult not to give in to a transfer of guilt from a member to himself, especially when he is not thinking clearly due to stress.

8
AVOID BECOMING A SACRIFICE

ONCE THE LEADER recognizes the potential of becoming the substitute sacrifice for others, he can prepare himself to manage any situation that might set him up for it. No preparation can absolutely guarantee this problem will be avoided. People may refuse to change. Some may ignore any help to take responsibility for their own lives.

A minister from Santa Barbara, California, learned the hard way how someone can refuse help. An elder's wife mentioned that she was having surgery the following week. The minister phoned and offered to visit. She explained it was a "female" problem which could only be corrected by minor surgery. She indicated that he did not need to bother. Therefore, the minister decided not to visit. Later, she expressed anger. She actually went in for a biopsy and wanted the minister to show more concern. Although the biopsy proved negative, she criticized the minister because her poor husband had to face the situation alone. In this instance, the minister received blame even though he had done everything that would be reasonably expected.

There are those who see how their lives can change. They will be open to suggestions. Through the power of the Holy Spirit in their lives, they will confess sins, repent, and become all that God wants them to be. When this happens, leaders achieve the goal of helping people to mature in their walk with the Lord and to live in obedience to Him. If this is our goal, we must do all we can to help people not rely on leaders, but completely on the Lord.

CHRIST IS OUR ONLY SACRIFICE

Knowing that Jesus Christ is the only sacrifice for sins restrains a person from making the leader a sacrifice. Scripture is very clear that there is no other sacrifice than Jesus. Only He can meet all the needs of mankind.

When Joseph doubted his betrothed wife Mary, an angel of the Lord informed him "She will give birth to a son, and you are to give him the name Jesus, because he will save his people from their sins" (Matt. 1:21, NIV). John tells us that Jesus "is the atoning sacrifice for our sins, and not only for ours but also for the sins of the whole world" (1 John 2:2, NIV). The Apostle Peter agreed when he wrote, "Christ died for sins once for all, the righteous for the unrighteous, to bring you to God" (1 Pet. 3:18, NIV). Finally, the author of Hebrews presents to us this truth: "By one sacrifice he has made perfect forever those who are being made holy" (Heb. 10:14, NIV).

An ever-present danger remains that people will look anywhere, other than Jesus, to find an answer to their need. Unfortunately they often look to the leader to fulfill this need.

One chairman of a pastor search committee said, "The church is not looking for a pastor; it is looking for a Messiah. We're overlooking the fact that the Messiah has already come."[1] Solutions to life's problems are found only in Jesus Christ. Jesus' finished work on the Cross is complete and capable of meeting every need, no matter how great. "The atoning work of Jesus Christ is infinite in value, and is therefore sufficient and efficacious for those who put their trust in Him.[2]

Anyone seeking counsel must be brought to an understanding that victory has already been accomplished in Christ and that any person who seeks forgiveness can receive His healing power.

To appropriate the victory of Christ, it is necessary to be dissatisfied with the present and have a willingness to catch and ride the currents that are moving to a more creative future. We can appropriate the victory of Christ by the cultivation of an openness to the power of Christ.[3]

The healing power of Christ can only be received when a person is willing to acknowledge his or her sins and that Jesus Christ is the only sacrifice for him or her. No substitute exists. Christ is the only lamb that takes away the sin of the world (John 1:29). Hulme elaborates this point:

> Letting out our anger on Christ as the lamb is thera-peutic. We can be aware of the process even while we are doing it...Letting out our anger on the lamb makes anger manageable because His sacrifice keeps us responsible. Scapegoating, however, feeds off into our self-righteousness. We justify our attacks on scape-goats, usually by making them seem less than human in one way or another. But, the lamb keeps the respon-sibility where it belongs, namely on us because we are responsible as fallen human beings for the death of Christ. "Our sickness" says Allison "is our destructive anger." It culminates in the crucifixion of Christ; "our medicine is God's taking our anger. If we do not give it to Him, we are not healed by it." Letting our anger out on the lamb prevents our warm anger from congealing into cold anger.[4]

CHRIST—THE FOCUS IN THE COUNSELING ROOM

We have seen that many leaders who are "set-up" assume more authority than God grants them. In a counseling situation, this tendency can even set them up to be a sacrifice. For this reason, it is especially important to keep Christ at the center of any counseling activity. Henning writes, "We want to say quite explicitly that it is the central mission of pastoral care to communicate to those in pain the message of the Cross and the resurrection of Christ."[5] Wayne Oates uses the phrase "third presence" to describe how Christ should minister in the counseling office. Oates also observes how placing the emphasis on Christ keeps leaders off of their pedestal.

> Shifting the focus of our counseling on the Third Person creates a fellowship of suffering between us and our counselee. Our common humanity with him/her replaces both our need to place us on a pedestal at best and to deify us at worst....What we do is done in the Presence of the Third Person, the Christ, Who died for this individual! Pastoral counseling done with an explicit awareness of the Third Presence of the Christ in relationship, then, creates a down-to-earth humility in the counselor.[6]

Once leaders see themselves as ones who, like their counselees, have been saved by grace they:

> ...can deal gently with the ignorance and waywardness of counselees because we ourselves are beset with weakness. We therefore confess our own weakness as we lead the counselees in confession to God.[7]

The primary place for the set up of a leader to become a sacrifice is most likely a counseling situation. Understanding this philosophy will certainly determine how one is to proceed in dealing with any individual who may attempt to set the leader up to become a sacrifice.

LOCATIONS OF THE SET UP

Even though a counseling situation can be the most likely location for a leader to be set up to become a sacrifice, it is possible that the set up can take place in other locations.

I met a man at a local restaurant one evening. He had phoned, frantic to meet with me immediately. The man was going through a great deal of trauma, and it was clear that he was under an immense amount of stress. His wife had admitted to him that she was having a homosexual relationship with an eighteen-year-old woman. During the conversation at the restaurant, he began to reveal information about himself and his wife that was very personal. He admitted how he and his wife had rented R and X rated media to enhance their love-making. He spoke of how he could use his father's influence to take his kids away and establish a new identity. He was convinced that nothing could stop him from doing what he needed to do to protect his personal interest. In this informal environment, I become the sin bearer. The man later expressed how he was dissatisfied with the church and began attending another church nearby. He believed the church had serious problems and the leadership was flawed.

The conversation that sets up a minister as a sacrifice may be even more informal than meeting at a restaurant. A brief conversation can take place in a hallway, in an office, or briefly in a parking lot at 9:00 p.m. In any location, the dynamics can be set in motion for sacrificing.

There are many places where the set up can occur, but the most likely is in counseling. So, should a leader do counseling?

9

SHOULD A LEADER DO COUNSELING?

I SHARED THE CONCEPT of the leader as sacrifice with a minister at a mission conference at Green Lake, Wisconsin. After a lengthy discussion, he asked a very important question. How much counseling would a minister be advised to do? How many sessions might be appropriate with a counselee?

This is clearly a complex question. Many ministers live in rural areas where there is no one else to counsel except the local minister. Even when professional counselors are available, ministers are often chosen over them. Other leaders who show the compassion of Christ will find themselves in positions where people will want to share their burdens.

People generally find leaders more accessible than professional counselors. The fee is also a factor. The price is right if you want to see a Christian leader you know. However, cost is not the only advantage for a person who seeks help. Fear of the unknown is less because the individual may already be in relationship with the leader. A leader is sometimes regarded as a friend. Often it is easier to take a problem to a friend than to a stranger. Leaders have another advantage over professional counselors. They have access to people and the people have access to them—often at any hour of the day or night. If difficulties arise, it is possible for a leader to address the matter, discussing the needs of that person. Leaders often have access to homes and have an ongoing contact with a person. This relationship can be valuable in monitoring progress.

The question remains, should a leader counsel? Several years ago, Richard Krebs wrote an article for the *Journal of Pastoral Care* entitled "Why Pastors Should Not Be Counselors." In this article he listed four reasons why they should not.[1] Since our assumption is that all Christian believers are ministers, I would suggest that these principles apply to all levels of leadership.

- First, people who come to the [ministers] for counseling expect an easy and quick personality change.

- Second, there is the danger of transference. In order for the transference to be complete, the [ministers} must be faceless. The [minister] cannot be faceless. Archibald Hart perceives a danger with transference. He believes that [ministers] "cannot afford the time and energy demanded by a counselee with a high potential for transference."[2]

- Third is the problem of role confusion. How can the [minister] be the master of ceremonies, the teacher, the moral example, and all the other roles a [minister] has, plus be the counselor?

- Finally, misplaced priorities can pose a problem. Which [minister] really has the time to do good in-depth counseling?[3]

Samuel Blizzard underscores this point. He writes: "[The minister] is expected to be a specialist. People who are confronted by a complex and chaotic world want to be counseled rather than receive a social call from the minister."[4]

When does the leader find the time to counsel or to adequately prepare to counsel? A professional minister is especially ill equipped to counsel. Krebs also suggests that being "a person's minister is as limiting as being a person's relative, or friend. Psychotherapists do not, or at least fairly quickly learn that they should not, work with friends or family members."[5] A leader must also realize that it may not be possible to be close to certain people. Archibald Hart explains:

> I know of some ministers who deliberately do not do one to one counseling; they want to avoid the closeness either because they perceive themselves as too needful of intimacy or because they are physically very attracted to the opposite sex and constantly have to fight off advances.[6]

I believe a leader should limit the sessions with a person, couple, or family to a maximum of two or three. Frequently, this may not be possible. Because of a myriad of other responsibilities and a general lack of professional training, a leader should limit himself to short-term counseling. This does not mean that the leader then eliminates all caring. The leader should always remain part of a "caring system" for individuals who are hurting.

PREPARATION FOR COUNSELING

If a leader finds it necessary to counsel or has determined he is gifted in this ministry, there are some preventative measures he can initiate in order to protect himself.

Dana Charry has studied the high priest's preparation for the Day of Atonement and noticed some principles that can be applied to the counseling room.[7] The high priest first separated himself from his family and his regular routine. He moved into the temple area and there became involved with the daily rituals of the temple. In a way, he practiced and prepared for the Day of Atonement. He removed himself from the daily pressures of life and prepared himself psychologically and physically for this important annual day in the life of Israel. According to the Mishnah, on the eve of the Day of Atonement, he surrounded himself with the elders of Israel. If needed, he received instruction. This was an act of humility for him. Although he held the prominent office of high priest, he was not to see himself as someone exalted, but rather someone chosen.

On that same evening, he heard from the elders about their great expectations of the coming day. Together they felt so moved by their expectations that they concluded their meeting by weeping together over what the awesome outcome might be. On the Day of Atonement, the high priest first confessed his sin and made sacrifice for himself. By doing this, he examined himself before ministering for the people.

These practices apply to the leader who does counseling. A leader needs time before entering a counseling situation to prepare himself. In a way, he must remove himself from the regular routine of life. The leader should understand he is chosen for this task. He is not holier or wiser, but God has selected him to serve at this particular time. Charry enlarges our understanding of this point.

> At the moment that he or she [the counselor] begins to feel inherently better, wiser or more virtuous than the client, the therapy loses its effectiveness, and deteriorates into exhortation or coercion. Before the therapy hour, this attitude of humility should be reestablished.[8]

The leader needs an "awesome expectation" for the things God's Holy Spirit can accomplish in the session. In order for a leader to approach the time with a humble attitude, he needs a balanced life, adequate rest, reasonable compensation, enjoyable recreation, a meaningful spiritual life, and satisfaction from family and friends. Finally, the leader must examine his own life to be aware of and to deal with his sins. This occurs so the leader can benefit the one in need.

Richard Hester offers leaders excellent advice they can use in the preliminary portion of a counseling session. If adopted, the leader might minimize the possibility of becoming an unwilling sacrifice. Hester developed the suggestions after noticing the importance of Old Testament covenants. While reviewing the nature of covenants, he isolated two principles he believed could be useful in the leader/counselor relationship.[9]

- First, covenants were a way of regulating human relationships. These covenants listed the promises of the agreement with blessings and curses.

- Second, the basis for the covenant is God. He is the One who has created the covenant parties and oversees the covenants.

The covenant is executed within a covenant community. This is almost foreign in a day when we emphasize individual freedom and the right to "do one's own thing." The ancient Hebrew thought differently. He viewed himself as part of the whole, whether that whole was family, tribe, or nation. Therefore, when a covenant agreement was completed, it was witnessed by those who were part of the community.

Applying this to the counseling relationship, we establish some modern covenant concepts. Those involved in the session list their promises for each other. These promises might include:

- the time and place of the meeting

- the issues to be discussed

- other persons who might be advised or consulted

- the commitment that decisions would not be made by the minister for the others

- sexual advances from either party will not be tolerated

- suicide plans will be set aside, and calls between sessions will or will not be appropriate

- not allowing the potential of the leader to be set up for sacrifice

Due to the context of community, both the leader and the one seeking advice clearly understand there are others to whom they are submitted. Obviously the session remains confidential, with an understanding that both parties are accountable to others. This truth helps prevent heroism, idolatry, transference, and countertransference.[10]

The biblical concept of covenant provides God as the paramount attendee of the counseling session. When God becomes part of the covenant, we say He will remain God and He is—

Not displaceable by any human "hero," that the human partnership of minister and parishioner has brokenness, suffering and sin on both sides, within [counselee] and minister alike, that in the relationship, both parties minister and are ministered to as instruments of God's care.[11]

Each person in the counseling situation understands that he is a sinner saved by grace. The leader agrees not to shoulder the responsibility for what the person does. Armed with a clear cut statement of covenant, the leader and the person move into a counseling relationship which has established boundaries that move both parties into God's purpose. The probability of the leader being set up for sacrifice is greatly minimized. A great advantage can be realized by taking time at the beginning of a counseling session to establish the perimeters of the relationship.

WHAT IS MAN?

The make-up of man determines our philosophy of counseling. Who is he? Is man the sum total of components? This is the historic view. The most widely held view of man throughout history is that he consists of two parts, material (body) and immaterial (soul and spirit). A popular view today is that man consists of three parts: body, soul, and spirit.

Each of these views contains weaknesses that are beyond the scope of this book. Each view, pushed to its ultimate conclusion, could cause a pastoral counselor to fail to deal adequately with the counselee.

Man can also be seen as a whole. The "whole man" view works best with the methods described herein. In the book *Christian Theology*, Millard J. Erickson calls the monism model of man "conditional unity."

> According to this view, the normal state of man is as a materialized unitary being. In Scripture, man is so addressed and regarded. He is not urged to flee or escape from the body, as if it were somehow inherently evil. This monistic condition can, however, be broken down, and at death it is, so that the immaterial aspect of man lives on even as the material decomposes. At

the resurrection, however, there will be a return to a material or bodily condition. The person will assume a body which has some points of continuity with the old body, but is also a new or reconstituted or spiritual body. The solution to the variety of data in the Biblical witness is not, then, to follow neo-orthodoxy's course of abandoning the idea of a composite nature of man, and thus eliminating any possibility of some aspect of man persisting through death. Nor is it a matter of so sharply distinguishing the components of man, as did some varieties of liberalism, as to result in the teaching that the immortal soul survives and consequently there is no need for a future resurrection of the body. In keeping with what has been the orthodox tradition within the church, it is both.[12]

The value of this view is man remains a whole. He is treated as a whole. When a leader counsels, he deals with the total person. He may at first see the person's problem as being an emotional, psychological, social, or a spiritual difficulty when in reality, it may be physical. Therefore, a leader might first recommend a check-up by the family doctor. I once was ministering to a person who was having great difficulty in life and recommended that the person have a physical. It was then that he discovered that his difficulty was a physical problem, not a psychological or spiritual problem. With medication, he was able to function normally.

Years ago, I dealt with an adolescent who did not believe God was real. Conversations about his faith suggested a non-loving or abusive family life. Could he have shut down his feelings in order to control his anger towards his parents? I realized he needed to deal with family issues before spiritual ones, which does not minimize the depth of the spiritual problems. This is an example how more than one issue may be present.

The wise counselor deals with all aspects of life. When a minister views someone as the sum of all his parts, the minister is able to more adequately understand how the different parts of the body, soul, and spirit interact. With the help of the Holy Spirit, the minister looks past the obvious to what may be causing the thoughts and behaviors.

Next, what steps can a leader take to keep from being set up as a sacrifice?

10

PREVENTING BEING SET UP
AS A SACRIFICE

THE COUNSELING SITUATION is fertile for setting up a leader as a sacrifice. So, what can be done to prevent this process from occurring?

Clearly, certain people will resist changing themselves and their behavior. In *Pastoral Counseling, A Ministry of the Church*, John Patton gives us one reason for resistance: "Persons resist change in pastoral counseling because they are fearful of some of the new things that they see and experience in that relationship."[1] Others resist because they really want a friend or someone to listen or approve. They are not really looking for counseling. Some want a quick fix—a way of dismissing guilt without dealing with personal sin and the need for confession and repentance.[2]

BE PREPARED FOR TRANSFERENCE

It is prudent for a leader to prepare for the possibility of transference in each counseling situation. The person might perceive the leader as a hero or god and begin the process of making him the sin bearer for his own guilt. Wouldn't it be great if preparation by the leader could insure that transference would not occur? Unfortunately, it can't. Samuel Bradshaw warns leaders about the dangers of transference:

> One pattern noted in several ministers consisted of difficulties incurred while doing pastoral counseling.

Like psychotherapists in other disciplines, the minister who had not taken special training is poorly prepared to handle the hazards of transference and countertransference processes in the pastoral counseling situation.[3]

Leaders might evaluate themselves as to whether they can handle the process of transference—even if they know it is taking place. James Davidson writes on the subject of transference in *Pastoral Psychology*. He convincingly states that those dealing with transference need a professional skill that most leaders do not have. He believes it would be better for pastors to be aware of the process, but to avoid fostering it when it occurs.[4]

Finally, once the mechanism of transference occurs, it is difficult for a person to recognize the process. Moshe Halevispero writes *"Transference as a Religious Phenomenon in Psychotherapy"* revealing that "there is required a tremendous step in psychological growth and courage before transference gods can be surrendered."[5] Simply put, the leader should avoid involvement in resolving the transference unless he has been suitably trained to do so.

AVOID THE PRESSURE TO DO SOMETHING

Another iceberg the leader must navigate is the desire to do something to help a person. A leader often hears of heavy problems. Compassion can move a lesser-trained counselor to help out. After all, help involves doing something.

"Do you need something? Go to a seminar or read a book and find solutions." Danger lurks for the leader who feels he must do something to resolve a person's problems. Doing something other than listening and giving biblical advice could cause the leader to set himself up to become a sacrifice. Instead of constantly doing, the leader should understand that at times simply being there is most powerful. William Hulme in his book *Pastors in Ministry* contrast being and doing.

> It is in the balance of the inner life with the other that we can understand and appreciate a ministry of presence. In our cultural values we are justified by doing. Doing is important also, in the Christian perspective, but it grows out of and does not substitute for being. Our basic gift—like God's—is the gift of ourselves, our person. In our culture, persons are what they do. We don't know what to do with a naked person. It takes the priestly balance to perceive the pastor as sufficient in being. A ministry of presence is the gift of one's person—providing comfort in the depths often unreached by actions alone.[6]

UNDERSTAND CONFLICTS WILL OCCUR IN THE CHURCH

In order to better understand the conflicts a leader faces, I conducted a survey of 108 ministers in California, Arizona, Nevada, Hawaii, and Kansas. The questions examined the emotional impact of conflicts and the results of those conflicts.

The participating ministers summarized a conflict that took place between them and someone else. They circled one word which most described the emotions they felt during the conflict. The possible choices of feelings were: antagonistic, disappointed, disheartened, pleased, furious, embittered, frustrated, hurt, annoyed, angry, hampered, delighted, and irate.

Many ministers listed additional feelings. These were: empathy, compassion, concern, and fear. One question asked how the conflict affected relationship with the member. They chose one of four responses:

the person(s) remained in the ministry, less active

the person(s) stayed in the ministry, no change

the person(s) went to another ministry

the person(s) stayed in the ministry but was divisive.

The final question addressed how the pastor felt as a result of the conflict. He circled one of the following: cynical, guilty, upset, dull, bright, angry, frustrated, discouraged, scornful, unconcerned, joyful (good learning experience), apathetic, sentenced, skeptical, indifferent, blameworthy, lethargic, pessimistic, suspicious, ashamed, sarcastic, or better. Pastors also listed as a write-in: careful, wiser, relieved, betrayed, unfortunate, sad, satisfied, sorry, regret, and protective.

Reviewing the surveys revealed conflict is common in ministries. Surprisingly, there were three who indicated they had not experienced any conflict. On the surveys, all others indicated a conflict had taken place between themselves and someone else. Negative emotions were generally felt during the conflict. Eight indicated positive emotions through the conflict. The others evidentially experienced much pain throughout the process of conflict.

On each returned survey many feelings were identified. The number of listed responses does not represent a direct percentage of the total. Itemized below are the "emotions" circled along with their total number of occurrences.

- disappointed—fifty-one

- hurt—forty

- disheartened—thirty-two

- frustrated—thirty-two

- hampered—twenty-seven

- angry—thirty-six

- annoyed—twenty-two

- antagonistic—seven

- irate—six

- pleased—five

- furious—five

- embittered—five

- delighted—two

- empathetic—one

- compassion—one

- concern—one

- fear—one

Reviewing the survey results reveals that intense feelings resulted from conflict. In almost all cases, the conflict was difficult for the minister. The survey also divulged that the conflict altered the relationship between the leader and others. Sixty percent of those who conflicted with the minister remained in the ministry but became less active. Twenty-one percent of those involved in conflict left and went to another ministry. Eleven percent of the people that were involved stayed in the ministry but became divisive. The ministers indicated on the survey that twenty-nine percent of those who entered into the conflict had other responses:

- The family stopped attending and requested their membership be moved to the inactive list.

- The person resigned from all positions because of dissatisfaction with pastoral leadership. He stayed and became much more cooperative and each of us held the other with more respect. Our relationship still seems to be strained.

- The deacons asked her to leave; however, the deacons who at first thought I was guilty, stayed. I was frustrated for one week while they assumed I was guilty until proven otherwise, yet not one confronted me face to face at any time, and I never even knew at the time what I was supposed to have done.

- I had to leave before the ministry split; many (40-50%) no longer attend.

- It took about six months of frustrated efforts before the person went to another ministry.

- The couple wrote a letter to the board and resigned all offices. They left the ministry and stated they would not return while I was the minister.

- The people did not return, and I left two months later.

- The person withdrew from the ministry for awhile, after knowing my resolve to remain as a minister and continue to serve. The member stayed away for a short period. He is now more active than before and recently accepted the position of financial secretary for the church.

- The person (and her husband) has stayed in the ministry and become more active and supportive.

- The man has since returned to our ministry and is much less involved six or seven years later.

- The individual left the ministry for nearly two years, and he is back in the ministry but not active.

- The individual displays an attitude of embitterment against the pastor.

- She has learned to live with it, but is not cordial to me.

- I left the ministry.

- There was complete reconciliation.

- They remained active and good friends.

Fortunately, it appears a Christian leader can enter into conflict and maintain an unchanging relationship with other persons. However only twenty-three percent of ministers indicated that those with whom they had conflicted remained in the ministry with no change in the relationship.

Some of the minister's emotions following the conflict surprised us. The ministers did not see all conflicts as negative. Many noted a positive feeling as a result of conflict. Thirty-eight percent indicated they found it to be a joyful, good learning experience. Thirty-six percent checked that the conflict caused them to be better off. Some, however, still experienced much pain resulting from the conflict. Of these, twenty-five percent indicated they were frustrated, twenty-two percent continued to experience discouragement, eighteen percent felt upset, six percent felt angry, and five percent felt cynical. Some noted that they felt much more cautious. Nine percent, for example, felt suspicious.

CONFRONT PROBLEMS:
CONFESSION AND REPENTANCE

If the leader notices during a counseling session or in other interactions, that an issue in a person's life must be addressed, it is crucial that the problem be confronted immediately.[7] To delay the confrontation can allow time for the leader or someone else involved to be sacrificed. Leaders are often inclined to avoid confrontation.

A study of Lutheran ministers reports that two-fifths of ministers tend to delay dealing with irritation and conflict and three-fourths are bothered by conflicts. Two out of three find it difficult to confront individuals about their moral and ethical responsibilities.[8] Why do leaders avoid confronting people about their sins? Some answers appear obvious:

- *The Need to Please:* Many leaders are so anxious to please others that they avoid confrontations.[9]

- *The Entrapment of Money:* The issue of money often complicates confrontation in organizations where funding is tied to donations. How do you confront the one who provides for you? As John Harris reveals, "We are reluctant to take risks with whatever gives us bread and belonging."[10] Once we "surrender here, then the next surrender is a little easier."[11] Avoiding confrontation becomes easier. One might ask, why endanger your future livelihood on a few principles?

Richard Walton lists a variety of other reasons that could hinder confrontation. These include:

- Internal forces such as attitudes, values, needs, desires, fears, anxieties

- Habitual patterns of accommodating

- External barriers, such as group norms against the expression of conflict

- Physical obstacles to interaction.[12]

Are there other methods of dealing with people? Is confrontation the only way? Yes, there are other ways. Their results are less satisfactory. Janice Harris offers three alternatives that can replace confrontation:

- The leader may turn against or actively abuse the other's beliefs.

- The leader may adopt other's values, denying his own.

- The leader may passively refuse to face any of the real issues which evolve as genuine differences between himself and others, effectively abandoning the organization to a life of discord and spiritual flaccidity.[13]

In a different approach Stephen Brown urges confrontation because other alternatives are not good. He gives to us four principles:

- The Principle of Waves. If you do not make waves now, a bigger wave will hit you later.

- The Principle of Image. People see you as a representative of God and will often react to you on a human level as they react to God on a spiritual level. When you are placed in this predicament you must take a stand.

- The Principle of Mandate. You have a mandate from God to lead and if you do not lead, your sin is unfaithfulness.

- The Principle of Passing. If you hold your responsibilities lightly, you can expect to leave quickly.[14]

11
GOALS: CONFESSION, REPENTANCE, AND FORGIVENESS

ONFRONTATION IS NOT used in order to single out a sinner for condemnation. Rather confrontation is needed for confession and repentance to occur. Hulme explains:

> The prophetic ministry naturally follows the priestly ministry. An example again is in pastoral counseling. Healing and becoming responsible go together. This is why confrontation is needed and in counseling, the pastor often needs to assist people to see what they resist seeing because seeing would imply the necessity for their doing something about it. However, when the confrontation is successful, a change in behavioral direction usually follows. In a broad sense, confrontation leads to repentance.[1]

According to Scripture, confession is essential in the process of forgiveness. In 1 John 1:8–9, it states clearly, "If we claim to be without sin, we deceive ourselves and the truth is not in us. If we confess our sins, he is faithful and just and will forgive us our sins and purify us from all unrighteousness" (1 John 1:8–9, NIV).

A leader should realize the great benefit to an individual when confession takes place. People have a need for confession. People need release from the guilt of sin. True confession can occur following a real sense of personal sin. Each person has to recognize the desperate nature of his or her own situation.

"To tear men from this impossible situation and to make them capable once more of receiving grace, God must therefore first of all reawaken within them repressed guilt."[2] Once this guilt is realized, man can make confession. The need for confession is clearly understood by man. Elizabeth Todd, writing on confession asserts:

> Man has [an] instinctual need to confess that which he perceives to be wrong or an offense against himself, against fellowman, or against God... Man's sense of wholeness and integrity and his sense of community are impaired if wrongs are not confessed.[3]

Confession itself brings about tremendous relief. "[Guilt] consciously recognized...leads to repentance, and the peace and security of divine pardon."[4] In confrontation the pastor seeks to launch an assault on the sin which holds a person captive. Such confrontation, when done in love, will not be fatal, but will rather bring back a person's integrity.[5]

Once an individual is made aware of his need to confess and repent, action is essential. Confession precedes repentance. To deny the need for confession and repentance would be like a dying person refusing a prescribed medicine that would bring him back to health. John Stott shows us the value of confession:

> Just so long as a person lives under the shade of real, unacknowledged, and unexpiated guilt, he cannot "accept" himself:...He will continue to hate and to suffer the inevitable consequences of self-hatred. But the moment he...begins to accept his guilt and his sinfulness, the possibility of radical reformation opens

up, and with this… a new freedom of self-respect and peace.[6]

The leader has an important role in understanding the art of confrontation that leads to confession and repentance. At this initial stage of confession, the leader functions as priest. Don Browning explains how the counseling environment encourages confession:

> There is an important sense in which the therapist helps the client make a confession that the client cannot make by himself…Therapy follows a sequence—empathetic acceptance, repentance (of conditions of worth) and confession.…Clearly it is the therapist's empathetic acceptance that helps the client to review and eliminate his conditions of worth and begins experiencing himself more completely. This is to say that the therapist emotionally accepts and owns (confesses) the client's unacceptable feelings slightly prior to the moment when the client begins to accept (confess) them himself.[7]

Browning points to Jesus as the perfect example of the way this process works. Jesus' confession before the Father of man's sin precedes man's own confession of sin. Man would not be able to make this confession by himself. Man senses the empathy of Jesus and this gives him the environment in which to make the confession.[8] We can see the danger in this process for the counselor. If the leader emphatically moves close to a person and does not help the person to focus on Christ for forgiveness, then the person may misinterpret the function of the leader and quite possibly begin the process of making the leader a sacrifice.

To understand this process we need to closely examine the actual structure of a confrontation session. The confrontation appears to take place in two phases, the differentiation phase and the integration phase.[9] During the differentiation phase, the parties in the conflict describe the issues that divide them. It is important that all sides of the issues be clearly understood during this phase. During the integration phase, the parties acknowledge their common goal and express positive feelings about the relationship. There may be one or more differentiation and integration phases in any one conflict session. It would be advantageous especially during the differentiation phase to make mention of the possibility of the pastor assuming the sins of the parishioner. Because we are speaking here of confrontation in the sense of confession of sin, the leader must also be careful to point to Christ as the One who can deal adequately with the issue at hand.

A THIRD-PARTY SOLUTION

If the conflict has continued for a long time, there may have been several confrontations in the process. Perhaps the leader has already been set up as a sacrifice, and the person is currently in the process of "crucifying" the leader or in making the leader a scapegoat. Emotions will probably be intense and thinking may not be as clear as under normal conditions.

One solution to this dilemma is to bring in a third party who can interpret to both sides what is taking place. Such a process might help a person come to the place of repentance, although, as we have mentioned before, there is no guarantee that this will absolutely take place.

If a third party is to be involved, the session must be carefully structured.[10] Before the first session, when both parties and the third party are present, there should be individual meetings with each party and the third party. When the first joint session is held, it should be in a neutral place agreeable to the principles. A location away from the organization would probably be preferable. The type of location should also be carefully selected. Serious thought should be given to the "formality" of the location. For example, a restaurant would be far less formal than a business office. The time limits should be known by both parties, making sure that plenty of time is allowed. It would be better not to fill up the allotted time than to have to break until a future opportunity could be arranged. It may also be necessary to add other persons (a process called intervention).

Finally, the third party needs to understand his role. He should be the one who initiates the agenda, restates the issues and views when appropriate, offers his own observations, and diagnoses what he sees happening in the conflict. He is the one who guides the process without manipulating the thinking of the principals. In other words he is one who has "no power over the future of the principles...but [does] have power over aspects of the process."[11]

STRESS-INDUCED AVOIDANCE

One fear common to those entering a confrontation is knowing it may be stressful. Fear or anticipated emotional trauma can preclude one from initiating the meeting.

Richard Walton reports that this stress, if it comes in moderate doses, can in fact help the individual to change. Evidently a person's "maximum ability to integrate and to utilize information occurs at some moderate stress level."[12] It would therefore seem prudent to address any issue of transference or projection that may result in the leader being set up for a sacrifice during the counseling session even if it is feared that stress will result. If the leader, because of fear of the stress of the occasion, would decide not to confront the issues at hand, he may lose a "golden moment" that could greatly benefit the person who has refused to deal with his sin.

We have seen there are certain people who will resist the possibility of a confrontation. Simply because the leader has a great heart and a deep and abiding desire to help a person, there is no guarantee the end result of the counseling exchange will be successful. Walton warns those who would enter into the confrontation to be prepared for some failure:

> Unless both parties have incentives for resolving or controlling the interpersonal conflict, the prospects for a confrontation are poor. Without adequate incentive on both sides, there will not be give-and-take in the sense either of emotional interchange or substantive bargaining and problem solving. If one attempts to engage another to resolve a conflict and discovers that the latter has more to gain by continuing the conflict, he may experience net losses from the venture.[13]

LOVE-MOTIVATED CONFRONTATION

Even despite the possibility of failure, a leader needs to confront. Such confrontation is an act of love. As Harold Brown has reminded us, we need to "love regardless. Christian love is not dependent on another's reaction."[14] Even if we fail in our confrontation, we have succeeded because we have attempted to handle the situation in a Christian manner.

THE POWER OF FORGIVENESS

Hopefully after confrontation, confession, and repentance, the parishioner will experience the desired forgiveness from the Lord. We have clarified that a person must accept, internally, forgiveness from the Lord for the sin of his life. Not to accept the forgiveness of God prevents a person from correctly handling his sin and opens up the possibility of spiritually dysfunctional options of managing his guilt. What is the nature of forgiveness and how can one know that he has been forgiven?

The Old Testament word for forgiveness, *salah*, has the primary meaning of "lightness, lighting up."[15] Psalm 130:4 reads: "But there is forgiveness with You, That You may be feared." (See also Exod. 34:7; Neh. 9:17; Ps. 86:5; Isa. 55:7; Dan. 9:9.)

The forgiveness that is offered must come from Jehovah Himself and is available for all sins except the sin of a "defiant and unrepentant sinner."[16] In the Old Testament, the notion of forgiveness is that there is no denial of the past, but rather a removal of the affects of the past.[17]

There are three New Testament words for forgiveness: *Aphiemia* originally "meant the voluntary release of a person or thing over which one had legal or actual control."[18] The word is used one hundred forty-two times in the New Testament and only forty-five of these times does it mean "to forgive." *Aphesis* means "to set free." While the word can denote "to set loose" as in setting loose a ship or to discharge an arrow, it can also mean to release from legal bond as in the case of letting loose from guilt or exempt from punishment.[19] In the New Testament, the word is used seventeen times and fifteen times it means forgiveness. *Aphesis* is used in Matthew 6:12: "And forgive us our debts, as we also have forgiven our debtors." (See also Exod. 34:7; Ps. 32:1; 130:4; Matt. 9:2; 26:28; Eph. 1:7; 1 John 1:7–9.) The word *parasis* is translated "letting pass or passing over, to let go unpunished." This word is used only in the New Testament in Romans 3:25: "God presented him as a sacrifice of atonement, through faith in his blood" (NIV).

There is immense practical application, which comes from understanding the word forgiveness. We can acknowledge that God and God alone is the One who can and does forgive. There is great relief in knowing that no sin lies beyond the grace of God except the sin of unrepentance.

When one feels forgiven, he feels lighter. He feels released from the guilt of the past. He understands there is now no judgment for what he has done. He has been set free to become what God has intended him to be. This is what man wants. He wants to feel the forgiveness of his sins. Nouwen in *Wounded Healer* has given us a poignant observation of our society's desire for forgiveness, "A fatherless generation looks for brothers who are able to take away their fear and anxiety, who can open the doors of their narrow mindedness and show them that forgiveness is a possibility.[20]

THE PAIN OF REPENTANCE

The process of forgiveness is not without pain. For one to reach the point of forgiveness, he must realize the need for repentance. As Paul Tournier explains, "Jesus does not awaken guilt in order to condemn but to save, for grace is given to him who humbles himself, and becomes aware of his guilt."[21]

The New Testament concept of repentance is to change one's mind. We recognize our guilt and make a decision to break with the past. "Forgiveness draws the curtain on the past, giving one permission to leave old ways and to enter into new ones."[22] This process can produce many moments of pain. The good news, however, is that once we turn towards the Lord, He can move with power in our lives. As Willut says, "Where there is even the slightest turning towards love on the part of the sinner, the redeeming flood is able to enter that person's life."[23]

THE ASSURANCE OF FORGIVENESS

How can we know we are forgiven? For many who confer with a leader, this is a critical issue. Many feel that their sin has been too great and therefore they are beyond help. Yes, they have asked for forgiveness, but are they really forgiven? This is also a crucial concern for the leader, for if forgiveness has not really occurred in the life of the parishioner, the leader can do little to assist the person. This adds another possibility where the leader may find himself being set up to become a sacrifice. James Emerson, in his helpful book *The Dynamics of Forgiveness*, equips us to respond to this concern of the leader and others. He writes:

> Forgiveness is not to be understood in any other than dynamic terms. To do so is to describe something other than what happens to an individual when he realizes forgiveness in his own life. "Realized forgiveness" is a dynamic that can be known not directly but by its results. One dimension of this dynamic is a context that allows one to be free. This freedom may be expressed as freedom from guilt, freedom to love, or freedom just to wait and see what must be done.[24]

The person must look into his own life to see if there is any evidence of the forgiveness he has requested. If he notices that he continues to be tied down to the past or if he is continually repeating the failures of the past, then it is very likely he has not accepted the forgiveness he has received from the Lord.[25]

Finally, when someone feels their guilt has come from interaction with a leader, they will find it difficult to forgive or receive forgiveness. It is at this point that he must understand where the leader's responsibility ends and his begins.[26]

12
AVOID SEDUCTION OF POWER

THE LEADER MUST be careful in the confrontation proce-
dure not to place himself back onto the pedestal. He
cannot be seen as the all-powerful leader who reigns
down judgment on others who apparently have not given up on
sin. The leader must come in love, as a servant, a sinner among
sinners, a beggar who has often come to the Lord as the person
now comes. This is no time to act like a Pharisee but rather a
time for humility and servitude. Richard Walton provides for
us a rationale for such thinking:

> Power parity in a confrontation situation is most
> conducive to success. Perceptions of power inequality
> undermine trust, inhibit dialogue, and decrease the
> likelihood of constructive outcome from an attended
> confrontation. Inequality tends to undermine trust
> on both ends of the imbalanced relationship, directly
> affecting both the person with the perceived power
> inferiority and the one with perceived superiority…the
> greater the unfavorable power differential, the less
> affirmative the attitude of the weaker person toward
> the more powerful one.[1]

One minister from Rolling Hills, California, shared a story
about a key man in his ministry, a chairman of the Board of
Trustees who made generous donations. The trustee suggested
that the pastor give some credit to one of the faithful elderly
deacons during the upcoming communion service. The pastor

agreed to consider it, but decided to stay with his policy not to name names during communion. After the service, the enraged trustee approached the minister, asking why the name of the senior deacon had not been mentioned. Harsh words were exchanged, both by the minister and the trustee.

At this time, it would have been possible for the minister to exercise his right of power and to declare that his way was correct. Wisely, the minister chose not to exercise that power. Later, both met together, had an honest conversation about the conflict, and apologized. The minister apologized for becoming outwardly upset. The session was ended with prayer and as the minister noted, a big hug. Because the minister was willing to become vulnerable at this point, it created the atmosphere for reconciliation to occur.

A leader who remains vulnerable is much less likely to be seduced by power. The Apostle Paul becomes our example as he admits to his struggles. "I do not understand what I do. For what I want to do I do not do, but what I hate, I do" (Rom. 7:15, NIV). Such vulnerability prepares us to be the best counselors. As John Harris emphasizes—

> Only [ministers] who struggle to become freer as persons in the company of others are free in themselves to assist others search for freedom. Put simply, that means to work at being continuously vulnerable to one's self and others, and in spite of painful defects, not to shut down, but to persist.[2]

This seems to be difficult for a leader. "We [ministers] can become defensive when reminded of our shortcomings."[3] This cannot be our attitude! We need to admit that we as leaders have limits. When we do admit limitation, we acknowledge that God alone can make up the differences in what we lack. Fortunately it seems that others are more open today to the fallibility of their leaders.[4] We have but to admit that we are vulnerable. Being vulnerable, incidentally, does not mean we "let it all hang out." When we say "vulnerability," we speak more of attitude. As Jay Kesler reminds us, any self exposure needs to have purpose. Just to express something, anything, to show how vulnerable we are is not the correct path of vulnerability.[5]

Clearly, servanthood does not mean passivity or weakness. To serve, we need not pull back when resistance is felt. Servanthood can be firm and directive. The warning of Stephen Brown can be applied. He writes:

> All too often in American churches pastors have become sitting ducks for neurotic church members (and they are a small minority). Somehow many have translated leadership into terms of servanthood and love that are divorced from the biblical sense of the words. As a result, a mild style of leadership has made them targets for every upset church member with a theological or cultural given. Such pastors could benefit from a Christian mean streak.[6]

A minister from Phoenix, Arizona told of the first serious conflict he had experienced in thirty-five years of ministry and in six pastorates. A young deacon who believed he was called into full time ministry gathered to himself a small group including two staff members. This deacon tried to undermine the minister and to convince others that the minister did not have as much authority as he thought he had. The minister was able to overcome the deacon's power play.

He said, "Many ministers are being challenged today, undermined, and criticized, etc. Only those who are strong and who defend their ministry will survive the ministry today! The stronger the minister, the stronger the ministry." The clear indication by this pastor is that while he is to serve, he must still exercise strong leadership.

DEALING WITH ROLE CONFLICTS

We have seen how role conflicts can help set up a minister to become a sacrifice. How does a minister deal with the role conflicts that he faces within his ministry? Smith in *Clergy in the Cross Fire* reminds us:

> One does not solve role conflicts by waiting for something to happen. One actively explores alternatives and methods of reaching a satisfactory solution. One takes the initiative to get the conflict out on the table so that those whose expectations are incompatible can resolve them either in direct negotiation with the minister or in discussion with one another, with the minister serving as a resource and help.[7]

Instead of increasing communication with those in which role conflicts are encountered, the natural tendency is to avoid and to decrease conversation. Unfortunately, when conflicts develop, we as ministers tend to withdraw from contact from those people.[8] Withdrawal is a self-defeating mechanism. When it is aimed at reducing role conflict, it actually initiates a vicious cycle that increases conflict. When one withdraws it cuts off communication.[9]

So what can a leader do? First, before a leader enters into leadership, he should carefully clarify the expectations of him. This "will presumably serve as liable insurance against an anticipated role pressure."[10] Second, he must understand "who he is, what he believes, what his understanding of the position is, what his values are, and where his strengths or weaknesses lie."[11]

Such careful thinking about his roles as a leader will help him deal with and understand any roles or expectation that might be thrust upon him. Such clear thinking will certainly help a leader to stop the process leading to a sacrifice.

THE GIFT OF LISTENING

The ability to listen is a remarkable gift that a leader can give to the others. "When a person has been listened to" says Muriel James, "he leaves the encounter knowing that his feelings, ideas, and opinions have been really heard."[12]

Listening can be a complicated process. Wayne Oates tells of a Finn who suggested that when a person says something, there are really three speaking: one that says what the person is saying; one that says what the person meant to say, and one that says what the person really meant to say. However, as Wayne Oates states, the number of persons really speaking could be endless. Somehow the leader needs to sort through all of this to determine what really is being said!

Careful listening in a conversation, with the help of the Holy Spirit, can provide the kind of clues that could prevent a leader from being set up as a sacrifice. Careful listening may also prompt the person speaking to really believe that the listener genuinely cares. There is then a greater likelihood that the person will open up and express the real issues in his life.

THE HIDDEN DANGER OF LISTENING

The hidden danger in good listening is that it could inadvertently set up a leader to become a sacrifice. As someone talks, he or she may be so overwhelmed by your interest that he or she may begin to see you as that person they always wanted to know. To them, you, as the leader, are the ideal person. With such interest in you, the person may be convinced that finally someone can help.

In a sense, you as the leader become an omnipotent person who cannot fail to fulfill their hopes and meet all their expectations.[13] Here again the issue of power surfaces. The leader could be easily swayed by the listener's admiration. If the leader falls to this manipulation, he ceases to be a good listener. Power has deprived him of the special gift of listening. If, however, he fights against the desire for power, he will provide the exact environment the speaker needs. Herve Linard de Guertechin writes:

> Liberating listening requires us to rid ourselves of the fantasy of omnipotence, which is the back cloth against which the other person makes his request. This shift of position, this "letting go" is an integral part of the process whereby we accept that basically we are as absolutely anything or nothing at all. We too share that suffering person's condition of weakness.[14]

QUALITIES OF A GOOD LISTENER

Finally, a leader will be a good listener when he has certain leadership qualities. What are those qualities? Warmth, genuineness, and empathy would be crucial. Gary Collins is more specific.

> The good counselor, for example, is able to get along efficiently, having a relative absence of immobilizing conflicts, hang-ups, insecurities or personal problems. The effective counselor is also compassionate, interested in people, alert to his or her own feelings and motives, more self-revealing than self-concealing, and knowledgeable in the field of counseling. The Christian might summarize all of this by stating that the counselor must be loving.[15]

USING THE TRANSACTION ANALYSIS MODEL

Transactional analysis provides another way of looking at the goal of a counseling session. Previously we looked at the transactional analysis model to understand how a leader can be set up to become a sacrifice. Using the same model we will answer the question: How can a pastor avoid being set to become a sacrifice?

It is the goal of transactional analysis to help a person operate in the adult part of his personality. In order to accomplish this goal, a person must learn to set aside inappropriate and irrelevant patterns in his current living style.[16] If he uses games of some type to manipulate others, he must learn how to recognize those games and find ways to give them up.

During the counseling session, the leader must be aware of how a person is acting. Jones, in *The Naked Shepherd*, warns the leader to take seriously the complex nature of a person's personality.

Every person is a complicated biological phenomenon filled with such powerful impulses and drives as dependence, self-love, competitiveness, envy, hostility, sexuality, and fear. When a person is insecure, holds grudges, or is inadequately loved, he usually demonstrates hostility in one form or another. Subsequently, a strange interaction of neglected love and hostility occurs. The ego is inflated and irritated. The victim of such formidable "forces" usually becomes increasingly aggressive or regressive. A minister must be acquainted with the dynamics of personality if he would effectively serve and safeguard his own health.[17]

Evidences of childlike behavior, especially blaming others, should warn the leader that he could be a set up to become the sacrifice. If that process seems to be in place, the leader may want to consider referring the person to a professional counselor who would be able to deal with the person's need. Not

105

to refer would seriously increase the possibility that the leader could become his sacrifice.

Using the Systems Theory Model

From the perspective of systems theory we have discussed the possibility that the leader could be moved into the family system and become the recipient of a blamer who would see the leader as the reason for his problem. The solution for this set up is to help people, both in the family and the leader, to speak in an honest and forthright way. In using this model, the leader should first of all speak honestly about his feelings. Second, the pastor should do all he can to help those in the crisis situations to also speak honestly. The difficulty is that our society does not encourage people to use this kind of communicating process. Thompson and Rudolph in their book *Counseling Children* write:

> Our society does not encourage people to use leveling responses. Although people would like to be honest, they are afraid to and play many games instead. Satir has outlined a variety of experiences to help family members to become aware. They can choose to change their responses and how they can do this if they are willing to accept the consequences. For them, such responses would not be the automatic response of people locked into a particular pattern. Levelers can choose to placate, blame, compute or distract; the difference is that they know what they are doing and are prepared to accept the result of the behavior.[18]

There is another approach to systems theory that moves beyond simply looking at the family as the system. In this approach, entire groups of people are seen as systems. This could include corporations, clubs, or churches. In viewing the organization as a system, one would not then look at a particular conflict as the real problem.

> System thinking helps us see that behind each problem there are many and varied forces at work…. casual forces are those that, taken together actually stimulate, trigger and maintain the way the system presently operates. If positive change is to be brought about, these "casual forces" must be addressed. "Intervening forces" are like the fever that accompanies pneumonia; they reveal that something is ailing in the system. To treat the high fever without treating the pneumonia that is causing the fever is to be dangerous and foolish. System thinking opens new options and opportunities for finding solutions that not only see how multiple factors are interrelated but also how solutions can be found that take these many factors into consideration and treat them as a whole.[19]

The leader who sees his organization as a system would understand that the complaint or accusation brought against him reflects more of a disruption in the system than on the problem that he as a leader might have. The leader is able to step back, and look and see what is going on in the organization that needs to be addressed rather than what is wrong in his life. Emotionally, this could be of great benefit to the leader. If his self-esteem is intact, which is central in Virginia Satir's concept of the system, then he is able to view what is going on more clearly. Evidentially, however, this is not a simple task. Key research carried on by Mennonite churches found that ministers do not think in such ways, but they tend to do the following:

> Take criticism from members personally rather than seeing it as a comment on the state of the church

as a system and the situation that the church has reached.

Accept member's evaluations as facts rather than viewing them as containing the member's own presuppositions, interpretations, and idealizations of pastors.

Seek personal relationship with members by moving outside their pastoral role rather than through it.

Place a higher value upon warm personal relationships with members than on keeping an eye on the system as a whole.

Accept inordinate and inappropriate guilt through allowing themselves to be identified as the patient (the sick one) in the system.

Think of ministry as serving people one by one rather than serving a complex network of subsystems all of which require ministry.[20]

The leader has to be willing to remove himself from the personal attack and view the entire system as it is functioning. This may be done by talking with others in the organization to see what their feelings are about a certain issue that he thinks might have generated the conflict he is currently experiencing. Candid and open discussions about the state of the church might help relieve the tension that has manifested itself in the attack by certain individuals.

WHEN NOTHING WORKS

What if you are the leader and all that you do to prevent becoming a sacrifice does not work? What if the person succeeds in making you a sacrifice? He then "crucifies you" and leaves the organization. How do you respond? You have a choice. You need not be crushed. You can choose the way you respond. Your attitude does not have to be that you are worthless. You can learn that the negative thoughts that you nurture are the actual cause of your emotional fluctuation and your sense of low self-esteem. These kinds of thoughts lead to depression and the desire to give up. Managing your thoughts will help eliminate these twisted ideas and allow you to return to a happier state.

As the writer of Proverbs says, "For as he thinks within himself, so he is" (Prov. 23:7). Maybe you have been blamed for something that is not your fault. But, what if some of the criticisms are true? David Burns instructs us that "if criticism is accurate, there is still no reason for you to feel overwhelmed. You are not expected to be perfect. Just take whatever steps you can to correct it."[21] If the person decides to give you an "exit interview" to work you over, you can respond in a positive way. Agree with the person wherever you can, avoid sarcasm or defensiveness, but speak the truth.[22] Such an attitude will more than likely diffuse the person, and will make it possible for reconciliation to take place at a future date. Notice how this works if you are a leader in a church. John Cionca in his *Leadership* magazine article entitled "Pastor, I'm Leaving" notes his five ways of coping with people who say they are leaving:

- Concede that people will leave your ministry.

- Praise God for diversity. Some will not like your style even as you don't like other's style.

- Look beyond the complaint to the concern. There may be a deeper issue.

- Accept criticism where applicable.

- Process your feelings with another person.[23]

13
HANDLING YOUR STRESS

T ODAY WE TEND to assume that stress is inevitable. It is a natural outcome of today's lifestyle. In other words, in today's society you will experience stress, and you need to know how to deal with it. Perhaps this is an error in thinking.

We first must define the word *stress*. Stress is "a physical reaction in the body." The purpose of stress is the body's way of dealing with the immediate physical demands of a situation. The body's reactions include increased pressure, increased blood flow to active muscles with the concurrent decrease in blood flow to organs that are not needed for rapid activity, increased blood glucose concentration, increased muscle strength, increased mental activity, and increased rate of blood coagulation. It is the body's preparation for either "fight or flight."

In the twenty-first century when a person feels stressed, his body is preparing for either fight or flight, yet he rarely engages in either activity. As a result, his body, which is now prepared for either fight or flight, must find alternative outlets for its stress response.

This brings up a question. "Do I always need to react physically to the circumstances around me?" If the circumstances require a physical reaction, obviously stress is good. If someone is chasing you with a knife, your body needs to be energized so that you can either fight or run. However, when we stress in a conflict situation, we are not able to utilize that physical reaction for practical purpose. Therefore we have no outlet for it.

This kind of stress can be very destructive, both mentally and physically. The reality is that we can choose not to react in such a way. Stress is not the only solution to our circumstances. We can choose to react in different ways. Richard Ecker writes:

> Humans can decide how they wish to react to their circumstances. The fact that we inherently choose to act like laboratory rats does not make us the same as rats. Unfortunately, we so often choose to behave like rats that it sometimes looks like we have no more control over stress than they do. But the fact remains we have the choice. We can, if we wish, choose not to be like rats.[1]

Every leader who is in a situation where he is being (or has been) set up to be a sacrifice can choose the way he reacts. He may choose to become emotionally involved and therefore react in a stressful way. That kind of physical stress will do its expected damage within the person's body and mind every time. A leader can choose, however, not to react in such a way. When a leader understands that he can be set up as a sacrifice, he then can move into a situation clearly in control of his thinking processes. When he observes that he is being set up, he can react in a controlled manner. Then stress can be avoided.

God's Power Over Stress

At this point, the leader has the power to choose. He may choose to be manipulated by his circumstances, or he may choose to accept the reality of the situation. If he chooses to accept the reality, he knows he is unable to control what is going on. However, a leader does have other resources. By faith, the leader believes God can intervene. This is not an easy assignment. As Ecker points out, "One of the most difficult truths to accept is the fact that stress prevention is only a matter of behavior."[2]

When that crisis situation occurs, we choose by an act of will to remember that God will keep His promises. These promises would include: "Cast your burden on the Lord, and he will sustain you (Ps. 55:22, rsv); "If you abide in me, and my words abide in you, ask whatever you will, and it shall be done for you" (John 15:7 rsv); "We know that in everything God works for good with those who love him, who are called according to his purpose" (Rom. 8:28, rsv); "My grace is sufficient for you, for my power is made perfect in weakness" (2 Cor. 12:9, rsv; "I can do all things in him who strengthens me" (Phil 4:13, rsv); "The Lord is my helper, I will not be afraid; what can man do to me?" (Heb. 13:6, rsv).

Support Systems for Pastoral Stress

When a leader has centered his spiritual life, there are other helps that can be used to handle the stress of being set up as a sacrifice. Any one of them alone may not be the final answer for the emotional tension that a leader is going through. A combination of a good devotional life plus some of the suggestions that will be offered could help sustain him or her in the difficult crisis he or she faces. A good beginning place would be to observe the findings of a *Leadership* magazine survey of one hundred church leaders in 1982. The question was put to the readers, "What support would be most helpful to you?" The following is a summary of the findings:

- Toll free support counseling services by phone.

- Periodic leader support seminars dealing with personal and professional needs.

- Leadership articles geared to needs.

- Personalized letter answering service.

- Peer support network in one's denomination.

- More personalized Senior Pastor/Associate/Staff relationships.

- Change of ministry.

- Having a professional counselor available at affordable rates.[3]

James Johnson in "The Ministry Can Be Hazardous to Your Health" offers his suggestions for handling stress:

- Take care of yourself physically

- Take a day off

- Exercise one hour a day

- Learn to say no

- Understand the authority structure in the church

- Delegate

- Learn how to run business meetings

- Do not take criticism as a personal put-down

- Cultivate one confidant in the church

- Establish close relationship with wife and children.[4]

Stuart G. Leyden in "Coping with Stress" offers his suggestions. He says we should:

- Adapt.

- Establish a diversion (do something else).

- Find a support group.

- Control your purpose in life. Know where you are going.[5]

Finally, Schoun identifies resources that should be followed in coping with stress:

> The resources an individual uses to cope may be called coping mechanisms or coping strategies. Examples include developing new attitudes, making decisions, taking pills, reorganizing time, prayer and meditation, physical exercise or diversions, sleep, and many, many others. The social resources of the support system may include relationships that are natural or spontaneous, e.g. family and friends…or they may be organized with intentionally appointed or sort-out helpers, e.g. clubs and associations having a common interest. They may be professional caregivers or simply fellow human beings.[6]

Knowing where you are going, according to Leyden, is essential to preventing stress. In defense of this concept, Leyden reports a very interesting study that took place in Stockholm, Sweden. In the Stockholm study, a group of train travelers were observed who had traveled by train a long distance. It was noted that those who traveled the furthest on the train experienced less stress, while those who traveled the shorter distance experienced more stress. In communicating with those who had traveled the furthest and the shortest, it was found that those who had traveled the longest boarded the train with the possibility of finding their own seat. Those who boarded the train later had little or no choice of a seat and thus increased the stress. The conclusion of the survey was that those who could be in more control of their life were more content. Pastors can therefore decrease their stress by formulating a clear idea of where they are going.

LIFE TRANSITIONS AND STRESS

The leader should also be aware that certain periods in his life are going to be more stressful than other times in his life because of his age. Transition times seem to be periods of considerable stress, and if these periods of stress were to be matched with conflicts in ministries, the likelihood of increased stress would exist. Schoun in *Helping Pastors Cope* notes three crisis periods in a person's life.

> In the age thirty transition, a person works on flaws and limitations of his current life structure. This person feels the pressure of making changes before it is too late. He may not have gotten into the career of his choice.[7]

Schoun notes that the next crisis time is mid-life. At this time "he may feel unfulfilled, disillusioned, bored or fatigued. He may question his accomplishments, begin to value other things and yet feel trapped. His marriage may be disenchanting."[8]

The final crisis stage is retirement when we begin to face the death of people who are closest to us. A leader should understand these transition periods of life. If he is in the middle of one of them, he can be aware that normal conflicts in the church may take on unjustifiable importance simply because he is experiencing specific emotional upheaval. Making note of that fact may prevent him from over-responding to a crisis.

Even in times of deep distress and stress, we can learn more about ourselves. A stressful situation can become the crucible that can forge in our life new dynamics of character that can be greatly used of God in the future. It is not unusual during a time of stress to simply react to pacify the external forces that are pushing against us. A more valuable approach would be to take the initiative and see what we can learn through that stress.

James W. Schut in "Coping with Pastoral Stress" suggests that in times of difficulties, ministers should make an honest evaluation of themselves.[9] Perhaps a respected person within the ministry or a trained counselor could help the leader identify not only what ministry gifts he really has, but to understand how those gifts can best function in his current ministry. Of course this means that the leader must be willing to listen to how he is being perceived. If the leader chooses not to listen, the stress most likely will continue for the leader and the entire organization could be affected. James W. Schut continues: "For the [minister] facing an intolerable situation, the [ministry] needs to find a workable plan which will rescue the pastor and the congregation from impending crisis."[10]

EXERCISE—THE FIGHT OR FLIGHT OUTLET

Another exceptionally valuable tool in handling stress is exercise. As we have seen earlier, exercise should be part of a person's attack on the stresses of life. Exercise adds the physical outlet for the fight or flight positioning of our body, which comes with stress. The importance of exercise cannot be overestimated. William E. Hulme has observed that people who exercise regularly often comment on how good they feel. Medical research has given us some biological information that would support this statement. It has been discovered that when a body is highly stimulated through exercise, the body produces endorphins which are chemicals similar to morphine. These chemicals stimulate the brain and the pituitary gland and result in a sense of well being.

We can handle stress by viewing life realistically. We must recognize that we live in a world that is not perfect and we live with people who are not perfect. "The positive minded," states William E. Hulme, "have come to a sense of peace over this issue while a majority of those who are hurting seem not to have done so. Instead, they often express disillusionment."[11] When we understand that our organization is made up of people like us, who are fallen, we can begin to view life as it really is. If we tend to be perfectionists, saying that everyone should be perfect, including ourselves, we are setting ourselves up for disappointment which becomes the groundwork of stress in our lives.

LEADERSHIP SUPPORT SYSTEMS

An extremely important element in dealing with stress is for the leader to find the kind of support he needs during his time of stress. Evidently this kind of support is not easy to find. Margaretta K. Bowers in *Conflicts of the Clergy* has noted "the [ministers] are lonely, set apart people."[12] Hers is not an isolated observation. Hulme has noted "both as individuals and in their marriages, [ministers] have a difficult time forming mutual friendships with other people and couples."[13] There are many reasons for this difficulty with ministers forming friendships. There can be a problem of a leader having a friendship with someone in his organization. Also, a lack of time to establish outside friendships does not make it easy to develop the kind of support that a leader needs.

Susan Harrington Devogel noting that ministers lack friendship, writes, "[Ministers] often find themselves with very few shoulders to cry on. The joys go uncelebrated, the pains go un-soothed, and the stresses go unresolved."[14] These words grew out of a survey of three hundred ministers in Minneapolis. Devogel discovered "that [ministers] were very reluctant to get involved with other people. Often this is because ministers had developed a lack of trust of other ministers and a sense of competition."[15]

Often a leader's solution to his frustration in finding support is to say that he trusts in God and allows God to be his support system. While, as we shall see, it is essential for us to be centered in God through prayer and in His word, it is also essential for us to have human support.

Ministers who limit themselves only to the direct help of God are not receiving the full help of God, and often this limitation is a signal that the person is somehow threatened by such human relationships.[16]

Scripture is very clear that we need to have this kind of support. Galatians 6:2 tells us "Carry each other's burdens, and in this way you will fulfill the law of Christ" (NIV). James instructs us, "Therefore confess your sins to each other and pray for each other so that you may be healed. The prayer of a righteous man is powerful and effective" (James 5:16, NIV). Paul reminds us to "Rejoice with those who rejoice; mourn with those who mourn" (Rom 12:15, NIV). He also tells us, "We who are strong ought to bear with the failings of the weak and not to please ourselves" (Rom 15:1, NIV). Not only do we have instructions to care for one another in Scripture, we have many examples. We are shown how Jethro was able to help Moses. (See Exod. 18:13–20.) Moses also received help from Aaron. (See Exod. 17:8–13.) Often Paul received encouragement and support from believers. Epaphroditus, Onesimus, and Titus were all men who provided support for the Apostle Paul. (See Phil. 2:25; Philem. 1:13; 2 Cor. 7:6.)

If support is essential to the leader's life, where should the support come from? An obvious beginning place for support would be within the organizational structure of the ministry. Unfortunately, even though many organizations provide an intentional program of support, often those support systems fail.

The reason for the failure seems rather obvious. Often the person who is directed to support the leader is also the one who is responsible for the placement of that leader into other ministries or is the one who would recommend that person to others. The leader is therefore reluctant to share his deepest hurts or needs for fear that information might be used by the support person to justify not recommending the leader for a new position. Even if there is some integrity to the support system of an organization, the leaders have expressed that they do not feel supported.[17] In an account by Jud of sixty-seven ex-ministers, twenty felt that they had not been at all supported, fourteen felt extremely isolated, and six felt the reason they had left the ministry was because of coercion by the organizational leadership.[18]

As a leader looks for support, he needs to be aware of the kinds of support that he requires.

> First he needs the "head patting" type of support. This is the support of consolation and encouragement in the midst of discouragement. Second, he needs the problem solving support which helps to analyze the stress and methods of developing strategy for dealing with the crisis that he is in. Finally, he needs the feedback support which allows him to understand how he is being perceived by others.[19]

Once a leader understands which support he needs, the task is to find it. Jud clearly exhorts the leader to find the support he needs:

> Meet more frequently with other [ministers]. Discuss your problems frankly and openly with one another; pray together; give to one another the helpful understanding and support which can best come from others who are facing the same difficulties, problems and frustrations. Plan together to talk over constructive programs and share with each other helpful suggestions which you have found to be of benefit. The [minister] must initiate this kind of support system. A few phone calls can rapidly help to form a group of support persons who will be willing to be with you, both in the good times and the bad times.[20]

There are many places where a leader can find the support he needs. Incidentally, he does not need to learn of these places by a hit and miss approach. The observations and experiences of others are there to assist him in narrowing down the possibilities that could best suit him. The research of Schoun in his report on a survey of 197 Seventh Day Adventist ministers provides a good source of information. In this survey several types of support systems were mentioned:

> Fifty percent of the ministers found that they could find the kind of support they needed in relatives (outside their wife) who they could confide in. Ninety-one percent of the pastors reported that their wives were a great source of encouragement and support to them.[21]

> Forty-five percent of the ministers found a great deal of support, especially early in their ministry, from older ministers. Ten percent of the pastors found support

from professional counselors. (Twenty percent of the pastors reported that they would have enjoyed professional counseling, but found it too expensive.) Twenty percent of the pastors found meaningful relationships with non- Seventh Day Adventists ministers.[22]

Career Development Centers are another excellent support system being made available to ministers. These are places were leaders can go for psychological and career evaluations. Many denominations have such centers. The American Baptist Churches U.S.A. has the Center for the Ministry headquartered in Wellesley, Massachusetts, and Berkeley, California. The United Presbyterian Church has the Northeast Career Center in Princeton, New Jersey, and several denominations have joined together to form the Church Career Development Council. (These facilities handle over 4,000 people a year.) These career development centers afford the opportunity for leaders to retreat from the daily pressures of their lives for a period of personal and professional evaluation. Such times of reflection and instruction help give leaders a more focused perspective on their lives.

Though there are several ways that a leader might deal with his stress, it is essential to understand that each leader is different. "No one type of program or structure will adequately meet the needs of all people, even in a closely structured system of professional peers."[23] Each leader will need to determine exactly what his needs are, and then move in an intentional program to meet those needs. Hopefully the concepts offered will prevent a leader from buckling under the weight of someone trying to sacrifice him.

Before a leader tries to cope with the stress in his life, it is essential that he isolate the primary cause of the stress. Often what he or she may interpret as the primary cause may only be a secondary cause. After the primary cause is identified, then a solution for the stress can be outlined. Andre Bustanoby in "How to Cope with Discouragement" gives some helpful suggestions for us:

• Look for physical causes.

• Look for physiological and psychological causes.

• Try to determine what is making you discouraged. Often discouragement comes because you cannot do what you want to do, cannot get what you want and need, feel guilty over something you have done or left undone.

• Express your discouragement openly.

• Determine if you are indulging in self-pity.

• Look for anger in your depression.

• Evaluate your thought life. Are you thinking positively?

• Experiment to see if you can break the spell of discouragement (by physical activities, hobbies)

• Don't permit yourself to fret with your depression.

• Determine if your needs seem to come in regular cycles. Chart your depression to see if it occurs on a regular basis.[24]

The leader can also deal with stress, very effectively, by entering into an intentional program of education. Schoun in his survey of Seventh Day Adventist Ministers found that eighty percent of those who had been involved in a doctor of ministry program found that they had reduced their stress and feelings of isolation and loneliness. Therefore, it would appear that any continued education, specifically a doctor of ministry program, can be helpful in refocusing a leader's life.[25]

NON-PROFESSIONAL COUNSELING[26]

Utilization of others in the organization is yet another way for a leader to prevent becoming a sacrifice. If within the structure of the organization a leader can provide opportunities for colleagues to be involved in ministry, there is less likelihood that the focus of attention will always be on the leader. Such a concept is certainly within a biblical framework. We are instructed in Ephesians 4:12 to equip the believer for ministry. When this kind of equipping takes place, then a leader can rapidly refer a person to either a small group or another trained person who can minister to the needs of that person. There is great value in the ministry of one member to another. Kenneth Haugk states:

> Christian care giving has significant advantages over any other method. The primary advantage is that of depth. I do not make this assertion lightly; it is the primary thesis of this book. Christian care giving is superior to care giving of any other kind.[27]

While that seems to be an extraordinary statement, other writers also reveal the great advantage of involving the entire body of Christ in ministry. Davidson has commented:

> [A pastor] can foster small groups such as teaching and talking-it-over groups. These provide wider networks for transference and depending upon the structure of

the groups, can provide such therapeutic elements as experience, experiment, support and insight.[28]

Since all are called to minister, there is really no area of support that should be outside the range of fellow Christians. Ronald D. Sunderland states: "There are few, if any, areas of pastoral care in which [believers] are inherently unable to minister."[29] Lawrence Henning sees "the importance of [believers'] support for one another instead of every person in the [ministry] depending upon the one representative of the one God."[30] Even the Roman Catholics are beginning to utilize more laity in the parish to minister to one another. Catholics are being taught today that it is the entire Christian community who has the obligation to bring God's reconciliation. The Catholic is instructed that when a person shares with you his guilt or his burden of sin, he may go directly to the Lord and ask the Lord to forgive his sins. "Healing and forgiveness are the ordinary responsibility of every Christian."[31]

Some might well argue that believers are not equipped to handle all of the dynamics of a therapeutic session. That observation is well noted. It is true that professional therapy is necessary in many instances. However, we should not write off the importance of non-professional ministry. Much of what is valuable in professional counseling can also be found within a non-professional counseling ministry, either in a one-on-one situation or in a small group. Janice Harris' observations give credence to this viewpoint:

> Responses to a questionnaire filled out by 131 patients who have received at least twenty-five psychotherapeutic interviews at a University Hospital outpatient clinic yielded a composite image of "the good therapist" as a "keenly attentive, interested, benign and concerned listener, a friend who is warm and neutral,

is not adverse to giving direct advice, who speaks one's own language, makes sense and rarely arouses intense anger."…psychological growth may be achieved in any authentic human relationship which makes use of the aforementioned qualities. Such authentic relationships may occur between lay persons and clients.[32]

It is extremely important for a leader who desires to avoid being set up as a sacrifice to initiate an intentional program of training within his organization. Such a training program would help equip the believer to do the work of ministry. The leader can, with full integrity, do this knowing that such equipping will make a difference in the life of his organization. The leader will at the same time help prevent a complicated "leader sacrificial system" from being formed.

REFERRALS

When a leader meets with a person, couple, or family the first time, he should begin to determine the issues that have brought these situations to his attention. If the issue is spiritual, then a course of action can be established and implemented. At this point it is possible to refer them to one of the prayer ministers in the organization for guidance and support. Sometimes it is not clear whether counseling is even needed. Perhaps the leader will need to consult with a professional counselor. Often it is possible to immediately refer the person(s) to the counselor. To facilitate the transition from leader to counselor, it is possible for the leader to make the initial contact with the counselor (although it would be preferable for the client to take on this responsibility). If needed, the leader can join the client and the professional counselor in the first counseling session with the counselor.

The leader should not necessarily end his involvement at this point. I have often given information to the counselor and if a waiver of confidentiality is given by the client, the counselor will also be actively involved in the discussion.

Maintain a Healthy Spiritual Life: Prayer and Devotions

Any crisis a leader faces will be guided in direct proportion to the quality of his private time with the Lord. It appears that the ability to survive a crisis without becoming discouraged or overwhelmed by the pressures of ministry is closely tied with one's devotional life. Having said this, the honest response might be, "Is this really so?" Does a private prayer time and time in the Word really make a difference? It most certainly does. William Hulme, writing in his book *Pastors in Ministry* interprets the results of a survey of Lutheran ministers. In the survey,[33] sixty-five percent of the ministers felt "so-so" about their prayer life; twenty-one percent were dissatisfied with their prayer life; and three percent were very dissatisfied with their prayer life. Another breakdown of the survey revealed that forty-one percent of this group was somewhat bothered about their spiritual life. Hulme then compared the spiritual satisfaction of the clergy with their satisfaction in ministry. The results confirmed what ministers have long held. A devotional life does make a difference. Hulme writes:

> The spiritually dissatisfied were more likely to feel dissatisfied with support they received from their congregation, to experience some serious stress about income, to be convinced that higher salaries would improve the lot of clergy, to be quite or very bothered by not having enough income to make ends meet, to be "so-so" to "dissatisfied" and to experience some

serious stress from perceived lack of freedom....Very
serious stress over "role expectations" of self and
others and frustration in conforming to expectations
is more common among pastors with a greater sense
of spiritual inadequacy. They also more often perceived
themselves as anxious to please others, and more often
are somewhat bothered by feelings they take their work
too seriously and by not being able to sleep before difficult days because they are too anxious.[34]

If it is true that leaders who are unhappy about their devotional life are more anxious to please others, one can see the
potential for a leader to accept the sin of others—in other
words, to become a sacrifice. It is therefore crucial to the spiritual and emotional life and the stability of a leader that he has
a regular and consistent quiet time. Hulme expands this basic
requirement to what he calls a balanced life. Such a balanced
life would consist of a twenty minute morning time of prayer
and meditation, a regular program of physical exercise, regular
social engagements twice a week, and a well-balanced diet.[35] In
other words, it is essential for a leader to take care of himself.
Some ministers, as Hulme observes, "tend to confuse their
calling with the need to live and sacrifice themselves, subju-
gating their own interest to the interest of others."[36]

The very center of this balanced life must be prayer. Prayer
is the stabilizing influence in a leader's life. Without prayer, a
leader's view of his ministry is distorted. Without prayer, the
pressures of ministry will overcome the leader. Without prayer,
exhaustion will finish off a leader. In this state, the leader is
vulnerable. Not only can he be set up to be a sacrifice, but he
can also find himself reeling from the backwash of the set up
by trying to deal with any given situation on his own, rather
than using the power God has made available to him. The leader
can be turned against or driven away when he tries to resolve

situations with his own power. All the emotional devastation that accompanies such a confrontation can occur and the entire experience can devastate the leader. Because of this spiritual and emotional havoc and the lack of spiritual life, the leader could find himself unable to discern the processes that are now in control of his life. He has become the victim. A new career may not be far away.

If prayer is essential to the leader's personal life, it is also indispensable in the counseling room. Real changes in a person's life will not occur without the work of the Holy Spirit. The leader is deluding himself if he feels he can overcome a history of unhealthy living simply through a few conversations. Wayne Oates encourages ministers to pray:

> Counselees can defy our every effort to enlist them in an alliance that moves away from destructiveness of their past sufferings and toward a new beginning in their lives. They "dig their heels in" and commit themselves to helplessness. This renders the counselor powerless. You can easily throw up your hands. You can lose patience. Or you can look past their fretful ragging. You can wait patiently for their basic dignity as a person made in the image of God to come forward. You wait. You pray that you may not wrong them...you wait upon the Lord that both you and the counselee's strength may be renewed. You ask that energy and hope will be provided for the time at hand and until you see them again. You ask for patience that your own frustration will not curdle.[37]

SURRENDER

While it is helpful to intellectually understand there will be some who will mistreat you, often that realization alone is not sufficient to sustain you when the conflict is bitter. Under the weight of a continual attack by others, it is natural to lose your bearings and collapse. At such a moment, simply trying to hypnotize yourself with reassuring words that "This is to be expected" may not ultimately do much to improve your outlook. This is when you need to remember the high calling of leadership, the high calling of service. This service is not simply carrying out the duties of a leader. It is an attitude of giving of yourself for the needs of others on behalf of the Savior. As Henri Nouwen reminds us:

> This service requires the willingness to enter into a situation with all the human vulnerability a man has to share with his fellow man. This is a painful and self-denying experience, but an experience which can indeed lead man out of his prison of confusion and fear. Indeed, the paradox of Christian leadership is that the way out is in, that only by entering into communion with human suffering can relief come.[38]

The leader, therefore, is one who gives of himself. Again, balance is the key. What has been said about balance in the leader's life previously is still important. Jesus is our perfect example. He gave of Himself, yet there were times He went into the wilderness for prayer and relaxation. Just because He did not expend all His energies every waking moment in service did not mean His entire life was not given to others. He did all He needed to do so that He could serve perfectly. We need to have this attitude of service.

14
LEADING WITH BOUNDARIES

I never wanted to be a golden bull, yours or anybody's.
I was content to adorn you as earrings to jingle when
you danced. I never wanted to be the center of your life,
the focus of your most suppressed emotions when you
danced around....I didn't want to seem strong and self-
sufficient and unneedy and omni-competent superman.
I didn't want to seem to promise to save....I wanted to
be your partner in the project....I never wanted to be
your savior, only your minister....I wanted to be your
partner and you made me your parent.[1]

YOU CAN FEEL the emotion, the heart, the pain that these
words represent words of a leader who had become the
sacrifice. These words express the emotions of a person
who simply wanted to serve the Savior and point others to Him
instead of becoming a scapegoat for the problems of others.
However, somewhere and at some time something went wrong.
In the process of life, roles have been confused, identities have
been taken, and assumptions have been made. In the confusion
of that moment, a leader who had desired to minister as best
he could, found himself in a position to receive blame for the
actions of another. A position that he, perhaps unknowingly,
allowed. Why had it happened?

As Ditter states, "I never wanted to be a golden bull, yours
or anybody's." A leader does not minister so that he will take
on the sins of others, but rather to lead others to the sin bearer,
to Jesus Christ. The idealism that first leads us into leadership

seems to see the issues more clearly in the beginning than those who have been in the leadership for a long time.

As one enters into leadership, he sees that his calling is to serve others. He is professionally trained, but his highest calling is to recognize that Jesus Christ is the only sin bearer and that without the shedding of blood of the Son of Man, there is no forgiveness of sin. The only answer for the guilt of man is forgiveness in Jesus Christ. Unfortunately no amount of preparation, no amount of study, no amount of philosophizing can adequately prepare a person for the complex dynamics that can occur in an organization's life. There is always a possibility the leader will become a sacrifice.

Sin has devastated people. Many are so guilty that they cannot adequately deal with the realities of their life. People are confused and disheartened. Although they sincerely desire to believe that Jesus Christ can offer the forgiveness for their sins, they find it beyond belief that it can actually happen. So they remain immersed in the miseries of life, not able to find the one who can rescue them. Much as a lifeguard who tries to rescue a drowning swimmer can find himself dragged down by the drowning person, so the leader who moves into the troubled waters of a person's life may find himself dragged down by that person. The guilt and sin that the person has not been able to deal with must find a rescuer. Since Jesus Christ is not given the opportunity to become the final sin bearer, the internal demands of the person to find a rescuing sin bearer forces him to look elsewhere. Those in positions of authority or leadership become the easiest target. The leader, because of his close identification with God, becomes an obvious choice.

The dynamics are established. The leader, who never wanted to become the golden bull for anyone, finds himself in the position of having other's sins projected onto him. In the course of life, a leader does not often sort through what has happened to him. Perhaps he doesn't know how to do so. He simply views this crisis as another in a long line of many crises in the organization. If his self-esteem is not intact, and his insecurities rule his life, he will eventually become so burdened with these projections and transferences that he will find himself unable to function properly.

Unfortunately, as we have seen all too often, many will leave leadership positions to move into other areas of work. Both parties have lost in the process. The person has lost because he has not adequately dealt with his sin and has not found the forgiveness that he so desperately wants. When he chooses to scapegoat his sins onto the pastor and leave the organization, or if he is able to drive the leader from the organization (both ways putting distance between him and the "scapegoat"), he has failed. He still needs to deal with those issues in his life so he might develop as a person and mature in Jesus Christ.

Leaving the organization never really deals with the issues in life because the central issue remains inside the person. Leaving the organization only moves the problem to another location and eventually the problem will resurface. The name of the scapegoat will change, but the process will remain the same. This person will still be deficient in character and never obtain the potential that Jesus Christ has for him. He or she will never experience the complete joy that can be found in Christ, and certainly their ministry will suffer. Their spiritual gifts will find little or no outlet and because of this, the organization suffers.

The second person who loses is the leader. If the leader does not understand the dynamics of what is happening, his discouragement will certainly affect his family and organization. The leader may find his enthusiasm waning, and, eventually, if he does not leave the organization, he will simply find himself performing a job.

There is no clear way to completely prevent a leader from becoming a sacrifice. However, the leader can seek to understand the components of the process and once identified, he can make adjustments and control his reaction to others. The leader can also help others to understand what is occurring and with skill lead others to unload their sin and their guilt on the Lord.

Leaders must guard against the tendency to become the god or father figure to the person. A leader must remain a servant. Finally, the leader must remain connected with the Lord. There is no substitute for a consistent prayer life. Constant communication with the Lord will allow the Spirit of God to keep us from becoming more than we ought to become and at the same time help us to become all that we can become.

Some two thousand years ago a man named John the Baptist was experiencing much success. Many people came to him and recognized his leadership skills and his ability to point others toward God. Many looked to him to be the one who would be the spiritual leader in their lives. John the Baptist, however, recognized that he was a way-pointer. He was not the way. John the Baptist could have easily established his own group of followers and maintained them simply by becoming another religious leader in a long line of religious leaders. He did not do this. He understood his function clearly. He was to identify the one who would become the Savior of the world. He was to identify the one who would become the final sacrifice. He was the one who would set aside self and power and popularity in order that the Son of God might have preeminence.

His words found in John 1:29 need to be found on our lips and in our minds when we find ourselves being set up to become the sacrifice. We must deny the role imposed upon us. We must refuse the power transferred to us. We must not assume the roles imposed upon us. We must rather point to Jesus Christ and declare that He is "the Lamb of God who takes away the sin of the world."

TO CONTACT THE AUTHOR

Aslan's Place
18990 Rocksprings Rd.
Hesperia, CA 92345

www.aslansplace.com

BIBLIOGRAPHY

Aden, Leroy. *"Minister's Struggle with Professional Adequacy." Pastoral Psychology 20. (1969): 10–16.*

Adler, Martin. *"An Analysis of Role Conflict of the Clergy in Mental Health Work." Journal of Pastoral Care 19. (Summer 1965): 2, 69.*

Anderson, George C. *"Who is Ministering to the Ministers." Christianity Today, January 18, 1963, 6–7.*

Anderson, James D. *"Pastoral Support of Clergy Role Development within Local Congregations." Pastoral Psychology 22. (March 1971): 9-14.*

Backus, William. *"A Counseling Center Staffed by Trained Christian Lay Persons." Journal of Psychology and Christianity 6. (1987): 39-44.*

Baker, Larry. *"Pastors Should Not Be Lonely." Arkansas Baptist Newsletter 13. (May 1976).*

Balebridge, William F. and John J. Gleason, Jr. *"A Theological Framework for Pastoral Care." Journal of Pastoral Care 32. (December 1978): 232–238.*

Bartlett, Edgar W., and John P. Koval. *Stress in the Ministry. Washington DC: Ministry Studies Board, 1971.*

Bartlett, Laile E. *The Vanishing Parson. Boston: Beacon Press, 1971.*

Bauckham, Richard. *"Weakness—Paul's and Ours." Themellos 7. (1982): 4–6.*

Beck, Aaron. *Cognitive Therapy of Depression. New York: Guilford Press, 1979.*

Beck, James R. "Christian Reflection on Stress Management." Journal of Psychology and Theology 14. (Spring 1986): 22–28.

Berkhof, Hendrikas. Christian Faith. Grand Rapids, MI: Eerdmans Publishing Co., 1979.

Berne, Eric. What Do You Say After You Say Hello. New York: Grove Press, Inc., 1972.

Blizzard, Samuel. "The Minister's Dilemma." Christian Century, April 25, 1956, 508–510.

Bloesch, Donald G. Essentials of Evangelical Theology. New York: Harper & Row, 1978.

Bowers, Margaretta K. Conflicts of the Clergy. New York: Thomas Nelson and Sons, 1963.

Bossart, Donald E. Creative Conflict Administration. Birmingham, AL: Religious Education Press, 1980.

Bradshaw, Samuel. "Ministers in Trouble—A Study of 140 Cases Evaluated at the Menninger Foundation." Journal of Pastoral Care, December 1977, 230–242.

Brandsma, Jeffrey. "Forgiveness: A Dynamic Theological and Therapeutic Analysis." Pastoral Psychology 31. (Fall 1982): 40–50.

Bratcher, Edward B. The Walk on Water Syndrome. Waco, TX: Word Books, 1984.

Broadas, Loren A. "Constructive Approach to Frustration in the Practice of the Ministry." Pastoral Psychology 22 (April 1971): 39–44.

Brown, Colin, ed. The New International Dictionary of New

Testament Theology. Grand Rapids, MI: Zondervan, 1978.

Brown, Harold G. "Trying to Save an Antagonist." Christian Ministry, July 1983, 25–26.

Brown, Stephen. "Developing a Christian Mean Streak." Leadership 8 (Spring 1987): 32–37.

Browning, Don S. Atonement and Psychotherapy. Philadelphia: Westminster Press, 1966.

Burns, David. Feeling Good. New York: Morrow Press, 1980.

Burton, Laurel A. "The Origins of Three Pastoral Perspectives." Quarterly Review 2. (Summer 1986): 64–74.

Bushnell, Horace. The Vicarious Sacrifice. London: Alexander Straham, 1866.

Bustanoby, Andre. "How to Cope with Discouragement." Christianity Today 21. (7 January 1977): 28.

_____. "Why Pastors Drop Out." Christianity Today 21. (7 January 1977): 14–16.

Caldwell, Taylor. The Listener. Garden City, New York: Doubleday, 1960.

Charry, Dana. "The High Priest, the Day of Atonement and the Preparation for Psychotherapy." Journal of Pastoral Care, June 1982, 87–91.

Cionsa, John. "Pastor I'm Leaving." Leadership 8. (Spring 1987): 98–102.

Claypool, John R. "Getting in Touch with Power." Quarterly Review 39. (1979): 12–18.

Corsini, Raymond J., ed. *Concise Encyclopedia of Psychology.* New York: Wiley and Sons, 1987.

Collins, Gary. *Christian Counseling.* Waco, TX: Word Books, 1980.

Davidson, James E. "On Transference." *Pastoral Psychology* 22. (April 1971): 21–28.

Devogel, Susan Harrington. "Clergy Morale." *Christian Century* 17 (December 1986): 1149–1152.

Dickson, Robert G. "Ministering to the Minister: Formulating a Program." *Reformed Review* 31. (Winter 1978): 88–90.

Dietterich, Paul N., ed. *Newsletter Church Letter.* Ardean L. Goertzen, "Pastor and People: A Complex Relationship Understanding the Congregation as a System."

Ditter, James E. "Confession of the Golden Bull: The Minister as Idol and Idol Maker." *Journal of Pastoral Care* 36. (Summer 1988): 205–217.

Ecker, Richard. *The Stress Myth.* Downers Grove, IL: InterVarsity Press, 1985.

Edelwich, Jerry. *Burn-Out—Stages of Disillusionment in the Helping Profession.* New York: Human Science Press, 1980.

Ellison, Craig. "Where Does it Hurt? A Survey of Church Leaders." *Leadership* 3. (1982): 107–109.

Emerson, James Gordon. *The Dynamics of Forgiveness.* Philadelphia: Westminster Press, 1964.

_____."Lay Pastoral Counseling: Thoughts and Response." *Journal of Pastoral Care*

291. (December 1986): 304–309.

Erickson, Millard J. *Christian Theology. Grand Rapids, MI: Baker Book House, 1983.*

Evans, C. Stephen. *"The Blessing of Mental Anguish." Christianity Today 17 (January 1986): 26–29.*

Foster, Richard J. *Money, Sex and Power. San Francisco: Harper and Row, 1985.*

Freeman, David S. *Techniques of Family Therapy. New York: Jason Arnson, Inc., 1981.*

Frye, Roland. *"Prince Hamlet and the Protestant Confession." Theology Today 39. (April 1982): 27–38.*

Furniss, George M. *"Healing Prayer and Pastoral Care." Journal of Pastoral Care, June 1984, 107–119.*

Gibson, Terrill. *"The Grace of Transference: God as Redemptive Process in Pastoral Counseling." Journal of Pastoral Counseling 16. (1981): 14–24.*

Glasse, James. *Profession: Minister. Nashville: Abingdon Press, 1968.*

Golden, Edward S. *"Management and Support of Church Personnel." Ministries Studies, May 1969, 26–28.*

Halevispero, Moshe. *"Transference as a Religious Phenomenon in Psychotherapy." Journal of Religion and Health, Spring 1985, 8–25.*

Harding, Leander S. *"The Atonement and Family Therapy." Anglican Theological Review 67. (January 1985): 46–57.*

Harris, Janice. *"Non Professionals as Effective Helpers for Pastoral Counseling." Journal of Pastoral Care,*

June 1985, 165–172.

Harris, John C. *Stress, Power and Ministry: An Approach to the Current Dilemmas of Pastors and Congregation. Washington DC: Alban Institute, 1977.*

Harris, R. Laird. *Theological Wordbook of the Old Testament. Chicago: Moody Press, 1980.*

Harris, Thomas A. *I'm OK, You're OK. New York: Harper and Row, 1967.*

Hart, Archibald. *"Transference: Loosening the Tie That Binds." Leadership 3. (Fall 1982): 110–117.*

Hater, Robert. *"Sin and Reconciliation: Changing Attitudes in the Catholic Church." Worship, 1985, 18–31.*

Haugk, Kenneth C. *Christian Care Giving, A Way of Life. Minneapolis: Oxford Publishing House, 1984.*

Hegel, Martin. *The Atonement: The Origins of the Doctrine in Catholic Church. Philadelphia: Fortress Press, 1981.*

Henning, Lawrence. *"The Cross and Pastoral Care." Currents in Theology and Mission 13. (1986): 22–29.*

Hester, Richard. *"Transference and Covenant in Pastoral Care." Pastoral Psychology 28. (1980): 223–232.*

Hiltner, Seward. *The Christian Shepherd: Some Aspects of Pastoral Care. New York Abingdon Press, 1959.*

Houts, Donald C. *"Pastoral Care for Pastors: Toward a Church Strategy." Pastoral Psychology 25. (Spring 1977): 186–196.*

Hughes, Kent and Barbara. *Liberating Ministry From the Success Syndrome. Wheaton, IL, 1987.*

Hulme, William E. *Managing Stress in Ministry. San Francisco: Harper and Row, 1985.*

_____. *Pastoral Care and Counseling. Minneapolis: Augsburg Publishing House, 1981.*

_____. *Pastors in Ministry: Guidelines for Seven Critical Issues. Minneapolis: Augsburg Publishing House, 1985.*

_____. *Your Pastor's Problems: A Guide for Ministers Layman. Garden City, NY: Doubleday and Company, Inc., 1966.*

James, Muriel. *Born to Love. Reading, MA: Addison-Wesley Publication Company, Inc., 1973.*

_____. *Born to Win. New York: Bantam Books, 1977.*

Johnson, James L. *"The Ministry Can Be Hazardous To Your Health." Leadership 1. (Winter 1980): 33–38.*

Jones, G. Curtis. *The Naked Shepherd. Waco, TX: Word Books, 1979.*

Jud, Gerald J. *Ex Pastors: Why They Leave the Parish Ministry. Philadelphia: Pilgrim, 1970.*

Kesler, J. *"To Unload or Not To Unload." Leadership 8. (1987): 72–76, 98–106.*

Krebs, Richard L. *"Why Pastors Should Not Be Counselors." Journal of Pastoral Care 34. (1980): 229–233.*

Leyden, Stuart G. *"Coping With Stress." Church Management: The Clergy Journal, January 1981, 14–15.*

Linard de Guertuchin, Herve. *"The Art of Listening in*

Pastoral Care: The Sources of Our Desire for Power." Lumen Vitae 41. (1986): 86–96.

Maguire, Max. *"A Case of Transference." Journal of Supervision and Training in Ministry 5. (1984): 75–76.*

McBurney, Louis. *"A Psychiatrist Looks at Troubled Pastors." Leadership 1. (Spring 1980): 107–120.*

McDonald, H. D. *Forgiveness and Atonement. Grand Rapids, MI: Baker Book House, 1984.*

McGinnis, T. C. *"Clergyman in Conflict." Pastoral Psychology 20. (October 1969): 13–20.*

Mills, Edgar. *"The Minister's Career Development." Improving the Practice of Ministry 1. (November, 1971): 13.*

Milne, Bruce. *Know the Truth. Downers Grove, IL: InterVarsity, 1982.*

Morris, Leon. *The Apostolic Preaching of the Cross. Grand Rapids, MI: Eerdmann Publishing Co., 1965.*

Nouwen, Henri J. M. *The Wounded Healer. Garden City, NY: Doubleday, 1972.*

Oates, Wayne E. *The Presence of God in Pastoral Counseling. Waco, TX: Word Books, 1986.*

_____. *Religious Factors in Mental Health. New York: Association Press, 1955.*

Oglesby, William B. Jr. *"Biblical Perspective on Caring for Careers." Journal of Pastoral Care 38. (1984): 85–90.*

Patterson, Ben. *"When the Alligators are Snapping, How Do You Operate a Small Pump at the Edge of the*

Swamp." Leadership 1. (Spring 1982): 41–46.

Patton, John. "The Pastoral Care of Pastors." The Christian Ministry, July 1980, 15–18.

_____. Pastoral Counseling—A Ministry of the Church. Nashville, TN: Abingdon Press, 1983.

"Psychiatric Glossary." American Psychiatric Association. 5ᵗʰ ed.

Richardson, Don. Eternity in Their Hearts. Ventura, CA: 1981.

Robbins, Paul D., and Harold L. Myra. "Conflict: Facing it in Yourself and in Your Church." Leadership 1. (Spring 1980): 23–26.

Sall, Millard J. Faith, Psychology and Christian Theology. Grand Rapids, MI: Zondervan House, 1978.

Satir, Virginia. Conjoint Family Therapy. Palo Alto, CA: Science and Behavior Books, 1967.

_____. Helping Families to Change. New York: J. Aronson, 1977.

_____. Peoplemaking. Palo Alto, CA: Science and Behavior Books, 1972.

_____. Step By Step: A Guide to Creating Changes in Families. Palo Alto, CA: Science and Behavior Books, 1983.

Schoun, Benjamin D. Helping Pastors Cope. Berrien Springs, MI.: Andrew University Press, 1982.

Schut, James W. "Coping with Pastoral Stress." Reformed Review 31. (Winter 1978): 82–87.

Short, Robert. The Gospel from Outer Space. San Francisco:

Harper & Row, 1983.

Smith, Charles. *How to Become a Bishop Without Being Religious*. Garden City, NY: Doubleday, 1965.

Smith, Donald P. *Clergy in the Cross Fire*. Philadelphia: Westminster Press, 1973.

Steiner, Claude. *Scripts People Live By:* New York: Banton Book, 1975.

_____. *Games Alcoholics Play*. New York: Ballantine Books, 1971.

Stott, John W. *Cross of Christ*. Downers Grove, IL: Intervarsity Press, 1986.

Sunderland, Ronald D. "Lay Pastoral Care." *Journal of Pastoral Care 42*. (Summer 1988):

Switzer, David K. "Why Pastors Should be Counselors." *Journal of Pastoral Care 37*. (March 1973): 28–32.

Thompson, Charles L., and Linda Rudolph. *Counseling Children*. Monterey, CA: Brooks/Coles Publishing Company, 1983.

Todd, Elizabeth. "The Value of Confession and Forgiveness According to Jung." *Journal of Religion and Health 24*. (1985): 39–48.

Tournier, Paul. *Guilt and Grace*. New York: Harper and Row, 1962.

Wadsworth, Allen P. "Drop-out From the Pastorate: Why?" *Journal of Pastoral Care*, June 1971, 124–127.

Walter, Richard P. "A Survey of Client Satisfaction in a Lay Counseling Program," *Journal of Psychology and Christianity 6*. (Summer 1987): 62–69.

Walton, Richard E. Interpersonal Peacemaking, Confronting and Third Party Confrontation. Reading, MA: Addison-Wesley Publishing Co., 1969.

Weeks, Gerald R. and Luciano L'Abate, Paradoxical Psychotherapy. New York: Brunner/Mazel, 1982.

Whitcomb, John C. 'Christ's Atonement and Animal Sacrifices in Israel." Grace Theological Journal, Fall 1985, 201–217.

Willut, Alfred. What the New Testament Says About Forgiveness. New York: Reflection Books, 1964.

Yancey, Philip. "Are We Asking Too Much?" Christianity Today 22, November 1985, 30–31.

NOTES
Chapter 1

THE LEADER AS A SACRIFICE

1. Edward B. Bratcher, *The Walk on Water Syndrome* (Waco, TX: Word Books, 1984), 9

2. Psychiatric Glossary, *American Psychiatric Association* (Boston, MS: Little Brown & Company, 5th Ed., 1980)

3. Muriel James, *Born to Win* (Reading, MA: Addison-Wesley Publishing Company, 1971), 38.

Chapter 2

IS SACRIFICE NECESSARY?

1. Robert Short, *The Gospel from Outer Space* (San Francisco: Harper & Row, 1983), 62–63.

2. Horace Bushnell, *The Vicarious Sacrifice* (New York: Alexander Straham, 1866).

3. Colin Brown, ed., *The New International Dictionary of New Testament Theology* (Grand Rapids, MI: Zondervan, 1978), 415.

4. Leon Morris, *The Apostolic Preaching of the Cross* (Grand Rapids, MI: Eerdmann Publishing Co., 1965), 43.

5. John W. Stott, *Cross of Christ* (Downers Grove, IL: InterVarsity Press, 1986), 91.

6. Paul Tournier, *Guilt and Grace* (New York: Harper & Row, 1962), 174.

7. Bushnell, 451.

8. Tournier, 174.

9. Don Richardson ministered as a missionary among the Donies of New Guinea. He experienced great difficulty in reaching these people for Christ until he found a custom in their culture that illustrated the need for someone to be given up so others could live. This story is found in Don Richardson's book *Peace Child*. Richardson has coined the term "Redemptive Analogy" to describe that story or stories in each culture that speaks of the Gospel. His second book, *Lords of the Earth*, is another story of Richardson's experience in New Guinea with the Redemptive Analogy model. His book, *Eternity in Their Hearts*, provides a general overview of evidences of Redemptive Analogy in various cultures through the history of mankind. Don Richardson, *Eternity in Their Heart* (Ventura, CA: Regal Books), 1981.

10. Martin Hengel, *The Atonement: The Origins of the Doctrine in Catholic Church* (Philadelphia: Fortress Press, 1981), 19.

11. Ibid., 28.

12. Tournier, 175.

13. Ibid., 179.

14. Ibid.

Chapter 3

WHICH ROOT WORDS DOES THE BIBLE USE TO DESCRIBE SIN?

1. Millard J. Erickson, *Christian Theology* (Grand Rapids, MI: Baker Book House, 1983), 568.

2. Ibid., 577.

3. Ibid., 578.

4. Donald G. Bloesch, *Essentials of Evangelical Theology* (New York: Harper & Row, 1978), 92.

5. Ibid., 93.

6. Bruce Milne, *Know the Truth* (Downers Grove, IL: InterVarsity, 1982), 104.

7. Bloesch, 90.

Chapter 4

WHAT DO WE DO WITH OUR GUILT?

1. Hendrikas Berkhof, "Christian Faith," *An Introduction to the Study of the Faith* (Grand Rapids, MI: Eerdmans, 1979), 193.

2. Milne, 106.

3. It is not within the scope of this paper to deal with real and false guilt. Paul Tournier's book, *Guilt and Grace*, should be consulted.

4. Erickson, 605.

5. Stott, 96. For additional thoughts on the awareness of man about his guilt see H. D. McDonald, *Forgiveness and Atonement* (Grand Rapids, MI: Baker Book House, 1984).

6. Stott, 143.

7. Morris, 45-52.

8. Stott, 138.

9. Ibid., 144.

10. Busnell, 451.

11. John C. Whitcomb, "Christ's Atonement and Animal Sacrifices in Israel," *Grace Theological Journal*, (Fall 1985): 209.

12. Stott, 146.

13. Erickson, 813. A further discussion of the use of *hyper* and *anti* is found in Stott, 147–148.

14. Bushnell, 39.

15. Stott, 161.

16. Ibid., 160.

Chapter 5

SOMEONE NEEDS TO DIE

1. Don S. Browning, *Atonement and Psychotherapy* (Philadelphia: Westminster Press, 1966), 123.

2. Tournier, 179.

3. Martin Adler, "Minister's Struggle with Professional Adequacy," *Pastoral Psychology* 20 (1969): 67.

4. Wayne E. Oates, *The Presence of God in Pastoral Counseling* (Waco, TX: Word Books, 1986), 3.

5. Charles Smith, *How to Become a Bishop Without Being Religious* (Garden City, NY: Doubleday, 1965), 13.

6. James E. Davidson, "On Transference," *Pastoral Psychology* 22 (April 1971): 21.

7. Browning, 150.

8. Halevispero, 12.

9. Davidson, 26.

10. Richard Hester, "Transference and Covenant in Pastoral Care," *Pastoral Psychology* 28 (1980): 225.

11. Ibid., 231.

12. Ibid., 228.

13. James, *Born to Win*, 245.

14. William E. Hulme, *Pastoral Care and Counseling* (Minneapolis: Augsburg Publishing House, 1981), 40.

15. Tournier, 139.

16. James, *Born to Win*, 245.

17. Browning, 255–256.

18. Ibid.

Chapter 6

WHY DO PEOPLE ACT THAT WAY?

1. James, *Born to Win*, 18.

2. Charles L. Thompson and Linda Rudolph, *Counseling Children* (Monterey, CA: Brooks/Coles Publishing Company, 1983), 161.

3. Ibid., 161–162.

4. James, *Born to Win*, 24.

5. Ibid., 26.

6. Muriel James, *Born to Love* (Reading, MA: Addison-Wesley Publication Company 1973), 82.

7. James, *Born to Win*, 29.

8. Ibid., 32.

9. Ibid., 87

10. Ibid.

11. Gerald R. Weeks and Luciano L'Abate, *Paradoxical Psychotherapy* (New York: Brunner/Mazel: 1982), 47.

12. James, *Born to Win*, 196.

13. Claude Steiner, *Games Alcoholics Play* (New York: Ballantine Books, 1971), 18.

14. James, *Born to Win*, 231.

15. Ibid., 234.

16. William E. Hulme, *Managing Stress in Ministry* (San Francisco: Harper & Row, 1985), 94.

17. Raymond J. Corsini, ed., *Concise Encyclopedia of Psychology* (New York: Wiley and Sons, 1987), 1103.

18. Virginia Satir, *Peoplemaking* (Palo Alto, CA: Science and Behavior Books, 1972), 112.

19. Ibid., 59.

20. Thompson, 127.

21. Ibid., 128.

22. Satir, 73–74.

Chapter 7

THE SET UP: A READY SACRIFICE

1. Lois McBurney, "A Psychologist Looks at Troubled Pastors," *Leadership* 1 (Spring 1980): 109.

2. Craig Ellison, "Where Does it Hurt? A Survey of Church Leaders," *Leadership* 3 (1982): 107.

3. Susan Harrington Devogel, "Clergy Morale," *Christian Century*, 17 (December 1986): 1149.

4. Aaron Beck, *Cognitive Therapy of Depression* (New York: Guilford Press, 1979), 11.

5. Leroy Aden, "Minister's Struggle with Professional Adequacy," *Pastoral Psychology* 20 (1969), 11.

6. James D. Anderson, "Pastoral Support of Clergy Role Development within Local Congregations," *Pastoral Psychology* 22 (March 1971), 9.

7. Aden, 11.

8. Bratcher, 28.

9. Laile E. Bartlett, *The Vanishing Parson* (Boston: Beacon Press, 1971), 52.

10. Margaretta K. Bowers, *Conflicts of the Clergy* (New York: Thomas Nelson and Sons, 1963), 3.

11. Aden, 14.

12. Bartlett, 71.

13. David Burns, *Feeling Good* (New York: Morrow Press, 1980), 181.

14. Ibid., 41.

15. Donald P. Smith, *Clergy in the Cross Fire* (Philadelphia: Westminster Press, 1973), 30.

16. John C. Harris, *Stress, Power and Ministry: An Approach to the Current Dilemmas of Pastors and Congregation* (Washington, DC: Alban Institute, 1977), 73.

17. Bowers, 10.

18. Bratcher, 24.

19. Benjamin D. Schoun, *Helping Pastors Cope* (Berrien Springs, MI.: Andrew University Press, 1982), 31.

20. Martin Adler, "An Analysis of Role Conflict of the Clergy in Mental Health Work," *Journal of Pastoral Care* 19 (Summer 1965): 70.

21. Adler, "An Analysis of Role Conflict of the Clergy in Mental Health Work," 73.

22. Donald E. Bossart, *Creative Conflict Administration* (Birmingham, AL: Religious Education Press, 1980), 102.

23. Schoun, 32.

24. Ibid. 33.

25. Aden, 11.

26. Bratcher, 33.

27. Jay Kesler, "To Unload or Not to Unload," *Leadership* 8 (1987): 75.

28. McBurney, 108.

29. Richard J. Foster, *Money, Sex and Power* (San Francisco: Harper & Row, 1985), 175.

30. Ibid., 82

31. Browning, 126.

32. Samuel Bradshaw, "Ministers in Trouble—A Study of 140 Cases Evaluated at the Menninger Foundation," *Journal of Pastoral Care* (December 1977): 231.

33. Smith, 30.

34. Devogel, 1149.

35. Lorena Broadus defines frustration as the "actual blockage of some goal oriented behavior...it is the feeling which results when a goal is not attained or not attainable at the desired time." Lorena A. Broadus, "Constructive Approach to Frustration in the Practice of Ministry," *Pastoral Psychology* 22 (April 1971), 39–44.

36. Hulme, *Managing Stress in Ministry*, 122.

Chapter 8

AVOID BECOMING A SACRIFICE

1. Bratcher, 184.

2. Whitcomb, 202.

3. Leander S. Harding, "The Atonement and Family Therapy," *Anglican Theological Review* 67 (January 1985): 55.

4. Hulme, *Managing Stress in Ministry*, 94.

5. Lawrence Henning, "The Cross and Pastoral Care," *Currents in Theology and Mission* 13 (1986): 26.

6. Oates, 123–124.

7. Ibid., 124.

Chapter 9

SHOULD A LEADER DO COUNSELING?

1. Richard L. Krebs, "Why Pastors Should not be Counselors," *Journal of Pastoral Care* 34 (1980): 229–230.

2. Archibald Hart, "Transference: Loosening the Tie that Binds," *Leadership* 3 (Fall 1982): 116.

3. David K. Switzer, *Journal of Pastoral Care*, Vol. 37 (March 1983): 28–32.

4. Samuel Blizzard, "The Minister's Dilemma," *Christian Century* (April 25, 1956): 508.

5. Krebs 232.

6. Hart, 112.

7. Dana Charry, "The High Priest, the Day of Atonement and the Preparation for Psychotherapy," *Journal of Pastoral Care*, (June 1982): 87–91.

8. Ibid., 90.

9. Hester, 227.

10. Ibid., 229.

11. Ibid.

12. Millard J. Erickson, *Christian Theology* (Grand Rapids, MI: Baker Book House, 1985), 537.

Chapter 10

PREVENTING BEING SET UP AS A SACRIFICE

1. John Patton, *Pastoral Counseling—A Ministry of the Church* (Nashville, TN: Abingdon Press, 1983), 181.

2. This article contains an interesting discussion on the importance of confession based on the Shakespeare play of Hamlet. Richard Frye, "Prince Hamlet and the Protestant Confessional," *Theology Today* 39 (April 1982): 27–38.

3. Patton, 181.

4. Davidson, 240–26.

5. Moshe Halevispero, "Transference as a Religious Phenomenon in Psychotherapy," *Journal of Religion and Health* (Spring 1985), 13.

6. William E. Hulme, *Pastors in Ministry: Guidelines for Seven Critical Issues* (Minneapolis: Augsburg Publishing House, 1985), 51.

7. This book gives a helpful definition of confrontation. "Confrontation refers to the process in which the parties directly engage each other and focus on the conflict, the nature and strength of the underlying needs or forces involved, and the types of current feelings generated by the conflict itself. If well managed, the confrontation is a method for achieving greater understanding of the nature of the basic issues and the strength of the principals' respective interest in these issues; for achieving common diagnostic understanding of the triggering events, tactics and consequences of their conflict and how they tend to proliferate symptomatic issues; for discovering or inventing control possibilities and/or possible resolutions." Richard E. Walton, *Interpersonal Peacemaking; Confrontation and Third Party* Consultation (Reading, MA: Addison-Wesley Publishing Company, 1969).

8. Hulme, *Pastors in Ministry*, 107.

9. Ibid., 108–109.

10. Harris, *Stress, Power and Ministry*, 115.

11. Ibid.

12. Walton, 75.

13. Janice Harris, "Nonprofessionals as Effective Helpers for Pastoral Counseling," *Journal of Pastoral Care*, (June 1985): 165–172.

14. Stephen Brown, "Developing a Christian Mean Streak," *Leadership* 8 (Spring 1987): 35.

Chapter 11

GOALS: CONFESSION, REPENTANCE, AND FORGIVENESS

1. Hulme, *Pastors in Ministry*, 125.

2. Tournier, 142.

3. Elizabeth Todd, "The Value of Confession and Forgiveness According to Jung," *Journal of Religion and Health* 24 (1985): 39.

4. Tournier, 152.

5. Janice Harris, "Nonprofessionals as Effective Helpers for Pastoral Counseling," 142.

6. Stott, 99.

7. Browning, 251.

8. Ibid., 252.

9. Walton, 105.

10. Ibid., 116–127.

11. Ibid., 132.

12. Ibid., 186.

13. Ibid., 96.

14. Harold G. Brown, "Trying to Save an Antagonist," *Christian Ministry*, (July 1983): 25.

15. James Gordon Emerson, *The Dynamics of Forgiveness* (Philadelphia: Westminster Press), 82.

16. Laird R. Harris, *Theological Wordbook of the Old Testament*, (Chicago: Moody Press, 1980), 1505.

17. Emerson, 82.

18. Colin Brown, ed., *The New International Dictionary of New Testament Theology*, (Grand Rapids MI: Zondervan, 1978), 697.

19. Ibid., 698.

20. Henri T. M. Nouwen, *The Wounded Healer* (Garden City, NY: Doubleday, 1972), 41.

21. Tournier, 114.

22. William E. Hulme, *Pastoral Care and Counseling* (Minneapolis: Augsburg Publishing House, 1981), 41.

23. Alfred Willut, *What the New Testament Says About Forgiveness* (New York: Reflection Books, 1964), 37.

24. Emerson, 72.

25. Hulme, *Pastoral Care and Counseling*, 51.

26. Burns, 199.

Chapter 12

AVOID THE SEDUCTION OF POWER

1. Walton, 98.

2. Harris, *Stress, Power and Ministry*, 75.

3. Hulme, *Managing Stress in Ministry*, 51.

4. Paton, 17.

5. Kesler, 75.

6. Brown, *Developing a Christian Mean Streak*, 33–34.

7. Smith, 109.

8. Ibid., 91.

9. Ibid.

10. Ibid., 84.

11. Ibid.

12. James, *Born to Win*, 48.

13. Herve Linard de Guertuchin, "The Art of Listening in Pastoral Care: The Sources of Our Desire for Power," *Lumen Vitae* 41, (1986), 86.

14. Ibid., 92.

15. Gary Collins, *Christian Counseling* (Waco, TX: Word Books, 1980), 25.

16. James, *Born to Win*, 263–264.

17. Curtis G. Jones, *The Naked Shepherd* (Waco, TX: Word Books, 1979), 78.

18. Thompson, 128.

19. C. L. Dietterich, ed. *The Church Letter*, Ardean L. Goertzen "Pastor & People: A Complex Relationship 2 Understanding the Congregation as a System."

20. Dietterich, 2.

21. Burns, 126.

22. Ibid., 128.

23. John Cionca, "Pastor, I'm Leaving," *Leadership* 8, (Spring, 1987): 90

Chapter 13

Handling Your Stress

1. Richard Ecker, *The Stress Myth* (Downers Grove, IL.: InterVarsity Press, 1985), 26.

2. Ibid., 82.

3. Craig Ellison, "Where Does it Hurt? A Survey of Church Leaders," *Leadership* 3 (1982): 108.

4. James L. Johnson, "The Ministry Can be Hazardous to Your Health," *Leadership* 1 (Winter 1980): 37–38.

5. Stuart G. Leyden, "Coping with Stress," *Church Management: The Clergy Journal* (January 1981): 14–15.

6. Schoun, 53.

7. Ibid., 11.

8. Ibid., 12.

9. James W. Schut, "Coping With Pastoral Stress," *Reformed Review* 31 (Winter 1978): 86.

10. Ibid.

11. Hulme, *Pastors in Ministry*, 90.

12. Margaretta K. Bowers, *Conflicts of the Clergy* (New York: Thomas Nelson and Sons, 1963), 3.

13. Hulme, *Managing Stress in Ministry*, 77.

14. Devogel, 1149.

15. Ibid.

16. Schoun, 83.

17. Ibid., 90.

18. Ibid., 105.

19. Gerald J. Jud, *Ex Pastors: Why They Leave The Parish Ministry* (Philadelphia: Pilgrim, 1970), 85.

20. Edgar Mills, "The Ministers Career Development," *Improving the Practice of Ministry* (November 1971): 13.

21. Jud, 14.

22. Schoun, 95.

23. Ibid., 94.

24. Donald C. Houts, "Pastoral Care for Pastors: Toward a Church Strategy" *Pastoral Psychology* 25 (Spring 1977): 191.

25. Andre Bustanoby, "How to Cope with Discouragement," *Christianity Today* 21 (7 January 1977): 28.

26. Schoun, 132.

27. Many states do not allow the use of the term *counselor* unless that person is certified by that state. Therefore you may need to use the term *Prayer Minister* and other such terms to identify one within the organization who counsels.

28. Kenneth G. Haugk, *Christian Care Giving, A Way of Life* (Minneapolis: Oxford Publishing House, 1984), 45.

29. Davidson, 26.

30. Ronald D. Sunderland, "Lay Pastoral Care," *Journal of Pastoral Care* 42 (Summer 1988): 168.

31. Henning, 28.

32. Robert Hater, "Sin and Reconciliation: Changing Attitudes in the Catholic Church," *Worship* (1985): 19–28.

33. Harris, 167.

34. Hulme, *Pastors in Ministry*, 35–37.

35. Ibid., 38, 43.

36. Hulme, *Managing Stress in Your Ministry*, 78.

37. Hulme, *Pastors in Ministry*, 155.

38. Oates, 40.

39. Henri J. M. Nouwen, *The Wounded Healer* (Garden City, NY: Doubleday, 1972), 78.

Chapter 14

LEADING WITH BOUNDARIES

1. James E. Ditter, "Confession of the Golden Bull: The Minister as Idol and Idol Maker," *Journal of Pastoral Care* 36 (Summer 1988): 205.